THE
Extraordinary
NATURE OF
Ordinary
THINGS

Steve Leder

BEHRMAN HOUSE
www.behrmanhouse.com

Published by Behrman House, Inc.
Millburn, New Jersey 07041
www.behrmanhouse.com

ISBN 978-1-68115-088-8

Library of Congress Cataloging-in-Publication Data
Names: Leder, Steve, author.
Title: The extraordinary nature of ordinary things / Steven Z. Leder.
Description: [New edition.] | Millburn : Behrman House, Inc., 2022. | Summary: "Rabbi Steve Leder reflects on the miracles of daily life in this reissue of his classic essay collection"-- Provided by publisher.
Identifiers: LCCN 2021042516 | ISBN 9781681150888 (hardcover)
Subjects: LCSH: Leder, Steve | Rabbis--United States--Biography. | Jewish way of life. | Conduct of life.
Classification: LCC BM755.L398 A3 2022 | DDC 296.092 [B]--dc23
LC record available at https://lccn.loc.gov/2021042516

The publisher gratefully acknowledges Shutterstock for the following images: 570560110, by suns07butterfly; 787197334, by HDesert.

Design by Zatar Creative

Printed in the United States of America

9 8 7 6 5 4 3 2 1

Contents

Acknowledgments

I am grateful to many people for their guidance in creating this book. I owe much to Rob Eshman, Gene Lichtenstein, and Marlene Adler Marks at the Los Angeles *Jewish Journal* for giving me the opportunity to publish often, and to Rabbi Bill Cutter for bringing my work to the attention of the fine people at Behrman House.

Without the help and good humor of my editors, David Behrman and Adam Siegel, this book would have floundered for structure and focus. Many friends also critiqued the manuscript at various points in its development, and I thank them all: Rabbi Harvey J. Fields, Hollis Glaser Ph.D., Susan Gordon, Mary Gwynn, Amy Handelsman, Peter Himmelman, and Gordon Stulberg.

A thank you to Bob Bookman and Ilene Rapke of Creative Artists Agency for their legal and business savvy. A thank you to Sarah Goldsmith for her marketing skills and to Steve Sigoloff, Hugh Milstein, and Don Weinstein for their artistry. A thank you to all of my teachers, including of course my parents and siblings, for educating me about books and about life.

Finally, a thank you to my wife Betsy and to my children Aaron and Hannah. They knew this book was a dream of mine and spent many days and nights without my attention in order for that dream to be realized. I love them more than words can say, yet hope I have somehow managed to say it anyway.

Foreword

In the fall of 1998, my phone rang. It was Steve Leder calling from the car on the way to the airport after addressing a Hadassah chapter in Washington State. An audience of four hundred, he reported, "They were in tears."

We were in the midst of preparing his first book for the printer. It was one of the early signs that even outside of the familiar walls of Wilshire Boulevard Temple, where Steve was then associate rabbi and is now the senior rabbi, he could move people, bringing them to laughter, to tears, and to moments of profound introspection, all with the power of a simple story.

Today his gift is no surprise to anyone. Steve has appeared regularly on the *Today Show*, on cable news, podcasts, radio, and in newspapers throughout the country. He has now published four books, and a fifth is due shortly. In the meantime, his congregation continues to grow—its spiritual and physical footprint expanding into new Los Angeles neighborhoods. No wonder *Newsweek* magazine twice named him one of the ten most influential rabbis in America.

But that outcome—his reach and influence—wasn't predestined, which is why it's illuminating to revisit these reflections of the young Rabbi Leder. He tells stories of the unfinished business lurking in the background of our lives— the emotional weight we bear from conversations each of us yearns to have with family and friends but too often avoid. We read of lives and opportunities for love taken away too soon—relationships cut short without the chance for healing and deeper love. There is Steve at the birth of a baby and at the bedside of the dying. There are poignant insights gleaned from his nephew's pet frog, his father's steel-toed work boots, a fishing expedition, an elderly couple in a Texas kitchen, and laughter about that same small town where he was introduced during his student pulpit days as "Rabbi Leder, the pastor from the Hebrew church." There are moments of deep reflection, sometimes joyous and sometimes sad. All these things become memorable vignettes that lead us forward on the path to a more beautiful and meaningful life.

We see ourselves in these stories. They make us laugh, and yes, they make us cry. They help us see our own lives from a new perspective; sometimes we observe our best selves and sometimes less than our best, and in that way, they make us just a little bit wiser. And if, as Steve likes to say, "nothing much is more than enough," then this collection of his early wisdom about the extraordinary nature of ordinary things is immeasurably so.

David Behrman
Millburn, NJ
2021

Introduction

*"Where does God exist?" the rebbe asked
several of his followers.*

*"Everywhere," the surprised disciples
responded.*

*"No," the rebbe answered. "God exists only where
we let God in."*

CHASIDIC STORY

At sixteen, as I traveled through Israel for the first time, my spiritual nerve endings were hypersensitive. Every face, taste, smell, breeze, stone, star, touch, glimpse moved me. Somehow I felt close to God, and now I was going to be closer —as close as Moses. I was going to climb Mount Sinai. Mount Sinai, the center of a believing Jew's universe, the time and place where Torah began, the Ten Commandments, God's thundering voice—soon I would feel it all.

That night, camped at the foot of the mountain in the middle of the desert, I began to feel weak. Something was physically wrong. I had ignored our Israeli medic's thickly accented advice that morning. "You must all the time drrrchink," he warned our entire tour group. "You must all the time drrrchink water. This is the deserrrcht."

By early morning, I had awakened our group leader, been examined by the medic and a doctor from the nearby army base. Dehydrated beyond the point of return to normal without serious intervention, I was given saline through an IV and driven several twisting kilometers through the desert to a base camp where I could recover and meet up later with my group. I would not get "Moses close" to God. I would not climb Mount Sinai. There it was, right in front of me, but I couldn't hack it. At sixteen, that kind of impotence sticks with you for a long time.

Of course, a lot has happened since then. Like most of us, my heart has been broken and mended by love. My wife beat cancer; others I love didn't. Being a rabbi has meant helping people celebrate and mourn, suffer and heal. I've watched my children being born, my parents age, my marriage mellow, a mission to Mars, the cloning of life, and the simple beauty of a family morning at home in pajamas.

At first, I regretted not making it up Sinai; now I realize that Sinai was only one place God spoke; a place, not "The Place." God, The One, The Eternal, The All-Mighty, is larger, better, deeper, higher, closer, simpler, more complex, and more present than any one place ... even a place as famous as Mount Sinai.

A two-thousand-year-old rabbinic parable claims that the Torah was originally given in seventy languages so that every nation could understand its wisdom and no people could claim it solely as its own. Long ago, the rabbis understood that God speaks in many ways—in nature, silence, music, love, and anguish. Our job is to listen in many ways. This is a book about how to listen, how to find meaning, how to find God.

Twenty-two years ago, the sixteen-year-old boy in me didn't understand how to listen; he was just sorry not to make it up Sinai. With time, I learned there is no single Sinai; Sinai is everywhere. Each of us makes our own climb: yesterday, today, and forever.

Steve Leder
Los Angeles, CA
1999

CHAPTER 1

"Where are you running to?" asked the Talmud professor of a young yeshivah student hurrying by.

"I'm rushing home to look over the High Holy Day prayer book before I have to lead services at my congregation," the student replied, trying to catch his breath.

"The prayer book hasn't changed since last year," said the old sage. "But perhaps you have. Go home and look over yourself."

CHASIDIC STORY

THE MEANING OF LIFE—no one can tell us where to search; no road map points the way. Still, to be human is to wonder about our purpose on earth. Every Rosh Hashanah Jews ask, "Did we manage to lift ourselves above our own petty concerns? Did we rise above the mundane and find spiritual fulfillment? Did we lead a meaningful life?" We call these questions *cheshbon hanefesh*, the scrutiny of our soul.

Since I use a Jewish pocket calendar every year, just before Rosh Hashanah I go through my own ritual of *cheshbon hanefesh* in a most graphic way. Before I discard the last year's calendar, I transfer all of the important dates I want to remember to the new year's calendar. I flip through page after page, week after week, month after month. The amazing thing is that I actually transfer so little of last year's information to the new year ahead. The birthdays get transferred year to year, the anniversaries, the *yahrtzeits*, the holidays. But the rest—the appointments, meetings, dinners, reminders, and notes—the tangle of activity with which I busied myself for an entire year, is simply tossed in the trash.

The only things that remain constant in my life, in anyone's life, are those sacred connections of family and friendships that survive year after year, generation after generation. It is a simple truth each of us knows. On days like Rosh Hashanah, the importance of family, friends, kindness, and love seems perfectly clear. The problem is that during the rest of the year we drift away from what really matters. We forget that every day is ours to fill...in our calendars and in our lives.

When we look back at the calendar of our lives, how many pages are worth saving? We schedule our business appointments—mastering the lessons of time management and efficiency. But do we really manage our time well? Have we celebrated with our children? Have we visited our aging parents and grandparents or made that phone call to the friend whose loved one is sick? Have we hugged each other enough? Do our children, our parents, our brothers and sisters, our partners in life and love, know what they mean to us?

Time is finite and insight elusive. Sometimes the search seems futile, lonely, and unsure. But if there is meaning in life—real, deep, eternal meaning—it is hiding in that force which drives us to be with each other. A child's smile, the warmth of human love, surviving pain, God's beautiful earth and its creatures, knowing that the music of our lives must someday cease—therefore how precious is the melody while it lasts—all of this is meaning, all of this is sacred, all of this can be ours.

It's a Boy

T hursday, May 25, 5:30 A.M. My wife, Betsy, wakes me with the words, "Steve, I think this is it." Rising slowly from the dullness of sleep, images swirl and converge into a whirlpool of simultaneous thought: "It couldn't be," I say to myself, "It's too cliché to be true. This happens to others, in the movies, on television, but not to me, not really." We time the slight contractions; five minutes apart for an hour. Our baby, ever so slowly, is edging his way into the world.

7:00 A.M. The hospital. Forms, drab, green gowns, and the most extraordinary sound. Betsy is attached to a fetal monitor, which puts out a steady stream of digital numbers and, most wonderful of all, a pulsating, unceasing rhythm, bleep after bleep, quick and clear. It's the baby's heartbeat, our baby, waiting to emerge from watery darkness.

The next eighteen hours are a surreal, sometimes frightening combination of pain, drugs, tubes, needles, boredom, exhaustion, and frustration. All the while, the monitor amplifies the steady, unceasing rhythm of the tiny heartbeat; charting each spasm, each yearning for life our baby has.

The drugs and the fear cause terrible shaking, and amid the shudders and the ache, it occurs to me that any real encounter with God, any glimpse of life in its primal, raw form, requires some pain, some pushing, screaming, and striving on our part.

3:00 A.M. Friday morning. Things are not going well. The doctor makes a decision. In an instant, Betsy lies strapped to the table in the cold, white operating room. Again she shakes uncontrollably from the drugs, the fear, and the sterile chill. It happens fast; the snap of latex gloves, gowns, masks, a rush of bright light, a flash of the scalpel, and then, as I lean over the makeshift paper curtain, I see a tiny head emerge from the crimson. A little, bobbing, wide-eyed head. Next a shoulder; pale, filmy skin; brittle, frantic arms. "A boy!" I hear myself shout, "Betsy. A boy!"

Suddenly, he flops out like a fish. "Dad, come here and cut the cord." In a daze, I obey. Rubbery and stubborn, it resists the stainless steel scissors. Then little Aaron is placed into my arms. "Congratulations, Dad," someone says. "Congratulations, Dad."

"Betsy, can you see him?" I ask, holding him close to her head.

The doctors continue to stitch. They cut through five layers to reach our son. Only then do I notice the blood collecting on the floor of the operating room. It is the brightest red I have ever seen; vital and powerful. The prophet Ezekiel's words come to me: "You shall live through your blood. You shall live through your blood." Birth, like revelation, is courage, ecstasy, and pain—demanding our passion and our blood.

The doctors peel off their gloves, and I know that Betsy will be fine and that Aaron, too, is going to live. For one brief instant, I grasp that love and life are really one and the same, that out of love grows the glorious urge to perpetuate life.

Walking with Abraham

The meaning of life is that it stops.

FRANZ KAFKA

Wednesday, August 16. Now three months old, Aaron is in the hospital diagnosed with whooping cough. A disease that kills a child every five seconds somewhere in the world. Our baby might die. We sit in the hospital room day after day, watching the downward spiral, watching life go on around us in slow motion. We assimilate doctors' words one syllable at a time because they make no sense, because we are exhausted beyond words, because they look at us with eyes that say, "I care, but I do not really care. I am sorry, but I am not shocked. I have seen this before, and I will see it again. He will probably live, but yes, he could die. Such things happen. It is only you who are surprised."

A fog, a dismal depression, a helpless resignation of our love and God-given right to parenthood, taken over by tubes, pumps, monitors, and needles. The infectious-disease department, with its gowns, gloves, and masks, has taken away even the right to touch his soft, peach-colored cheek; to kiss him on that little spot where his neck wrinkles in the sweetest way, or to rub his tummy, just the way he likes it.

I do the strangest things—make fictitious funeral plans in my head, imagining a tiny coffin in a tiny grave. I consider, for only the briefest fraction in time, life without him. I understand that my son could die, or live, depending upon a power so mysterious, so deeply hidden in the fabric of the universe, that most people glimpse it seldom, if ever, in a lifetime. I have become a conscious part of the unceasing rhythm to which all things dance. I really understand how sweet the music, how precious, how slender and melting, can be this gift called life.

For all my years of study, I never really understood why the rabbis commanded Jews to begin each New Year by reading the story of Abraham preparing to sacrifice his son Isaac. Why revisit such a grim, frightening tale on a day devoted to hope for the future? It wasn't until my own son was in danger that I figured it out.

Aaron survived. Still, his illness made me realize that most people never have to face the real possibility of their child dying before their eyes. That's why the rabbis command us to hear Abraham's story and walk in his footsteps as we begin each New Year. They use the Torah's saddest scene to remind us of what a gift it is to touch and hold our children, brothers and sisters, parents, spouses, and friends. Realizing that the people we love can die is to understand what it means that they live; holding them is to grasp the meaning of life.

Lazy

God has a purpose for everything, even a snake,
even a gnat, even a frog.

GENESIS RABBAH

"A useless pet that does nothing but float in poopie water all day" is how my sister, Marilyn, describes her son Matthew's pet frog, Lazy. Marilyn agreed to buy Lazy for Matthew ten years ago when, as a determined third-grader, he told her he really wanted a frog. At first, Matthew's prospects looked grim. The only frogs sold in Milwaukee pet stores required a steady diet of either live crickets or bloodworms. Marilyn wasn't breeding either in her house. There would be no frog.

But Matthew persisted, and after some research, Marilyn discovered Grow-A-Frog; a neat little establishment that mails you a tadpole that evolves into a hybrid African frog. Unlike its American frog cousins, this African variety could subsist on dried food pellets and remain in water its entire life. Having observed it many times, if you ask me, hybrid is far too kind a word for this creature. Basically, it's a fat, slimy, ugly thing that stares out of a little plastic aquarium and does nothing, absolutely nothing. Hence, Matthew's decision to name his plump amphibious friend "Lazy."

Lazy has escaped death several times in his ten years as part of my sister's family. Once, while my brother-in-law, Bob, was changing the water in the aquarium, Lazy slithered out into the sink and down the garbage disposal. Bob's hand was too big to reach in and rescue Lazy, and everyone else in the family was out of town. Bob had to stay up all night dechlorinating water and pouring it into the disposal so Lazy wouldn't crisp up. When morning finally came, he called a plumber to disassemble the pipes.

Then there was the time Lazy plopped out of his container and slimed his way under the microwave. Matthew picked up the microwave and told Marilyn to grab Lazy, but when the moment of truth arrived, she was too grossed out to touch him. Matthew did a quick hand-off of the microwave and tried to catch Lazy himself. In the meantime, Lazy slimed the entire kitchen while the dog tried to eat him, and my sister screamed from her perch on top of a chair.

Matthew could just dump Lazy in the pond across the street from his house and be done with it. But he knows that, being an African frog, Lazy would be a goner come winter. He could put him up for adoption, but Matthew's parents won't hear of it—not because they like the "wretched creature," as my sister calls him, but because they are trying to teach Matthew a lesson.

At eight years old, Matthew agreed to be responsible for a living creature, and that responsibility, as Marilyn puts it, "is not something you flush, give, dump, or throw away." Lazy, in all his floating, poopie glory, is Matthew's until he croaks— I mean, dies. Which, according to the woman at Grow-A-Frog who sells the food pellets, might not be for another ten or fifteen years.

All of this might sound silly to some, but to me, it's very Jewish. It's a lot like the rabbinic folk tale connected to the Torah portion about Creation. According to the story, when God created Adam, he was led around the Garden of Eden and told, "Behold, My works! See how beautiful they are. . . . Do not spoil and destroy My world; for if you do, there will be no one to repair it after you."

Anyone who's studied a little Torah knows that in the story of Creation, God grants human beings "dominion" over all things. The rabbis go on to teach that for Jews, dominion is not so much a privilege as it is a responsibility; that if we ruin the earth, if we forget that everything has a purpose, not even God can save us. How wise of the rabbis to warn us about our responsibility for God's creatures. How wise of my sister to raise a son who will not turn his back on a single one of them.

A Leap of Faith

When you must, you can.

YIDDISH PROVERB

Being the staff member in charge, I had to set a good example as the temple's men's group took on the Ropes Challenge Course at our camp in Malibu. Picture a series of thirty- to sixty-foot poles, heavy cables, dangling ropes, and suspended platforms. Now picture twenty slightly overweight, overdressed guys staring up at all that hardware trying to disguise the fact that this whole thing scares them more than an audit by the IRS. The facilitator, a huge, chiseled-looking man who has dealt with wimps like us before, assures us that if we work together, we can overcome every obstacle. "Now harness up!" he shouts.

The straps around my thighs and under my arms, the buckles and latches across my chest, and a single steel loop in the back attached to a rope are what will save my life if I fall. Ever the good leader, I agree to go first. My task? To climb a thirty-foot telephone pole, stand on the very top, and then leap into the air reaching for a small bell suspended on a cable ten feet out and above my head. After ringing the bell, I'll free-fall until my partners pull the rope connected to my harness. Theoretically, this "challenge" requires the same kind of courage needed to face the real challenges in my life. Halfway up the pole, I am unconvinced.

Reaching the top, I marvel at the surrounding trees glittering in the sun. At one with the shimmering rush, I begin to focus. Pulling my chest above the last hand grip, gently lifting one foot atop the pole onto the small circle of wood that would be my launching pad, I freeze. In order to move my other foot onto the top of the pole, I have to balance on the foot already there and let go with both hands. Let go with both hands? I cannot do it. I cannot look down. I cannot move.

The longer I search for a different option, the more apparent it becomes that the only way to stand on the pole is to first let go with my hands. But to let go with my hands is to risk falling. This is the real thing. There is no one to help me and no one to call it quits. In a moment of inner truth I decide that I am brave, that I am not a loser. I will never climb down the pole defeated; I will either stand straight at the top and leap off in glory, or fall trying. Metaphysics must conquer physics. I cannot let go, but I must let go.

Loosening my hands with the deliberate motion of a tai chi master, balancing on one foot, I let go as I ease the other foot up. Rising from my crouched position as carefully as a flower unfolding, I stand upright on top of the swaying pole. I have done it. But still, the bell hangs, beckons, dares, from ten feet in front and above me. To ring it, I have to leap out and fly like Superman—if only for a second.

I cannot hear my partners on the ground, the wind, the birds, or the rustling leaves. My universe is silent and empty except for two things—the bell and my struggle to believe. In focused madness, I launch myself through the air. Each moment is framed and separate, the bending, the leaping, a slow extending of the arm, fingers uncurling, the swing of the rope and the sound of the bell (I must have hit it), free-falling, the jerk of the harness around my chest.

I hear sounds again—as if someone clicked off the mute button—shouting, clapping, cheering. Being lowered steadily to the ground like a spider descending its web, I watch the guys gather below to welcome me back to earth. With Chasidic-like clarity, I realize that freedom is the conquering of fear. I am transformed.

Now I realize why our ancestors who worshiped the golden calf never made it to the Promised Land. When Moses was a day late coming back from Mount Sinai, they reverted to their slave past and their idolatry, dancing around, frenzied, afraid and faithless—believing they were lost instead of believing in themselves. What a different story it would have been had they decided to look not to a golden calf but to each other to calm their fears and to lessen their loneliness. What a different lesson we would learn if they had held each others' hands and climbed bravely up the mountain to search for Moses and God, instead of running scared.

Oh, I know that this was just a Sunday afternoon with the guys. And I know that a pole and a bell are nothing but wood and metal. But suppose they are something more too. Suppose they are metaphors for the two choices our ancestors had in their lives and we have in ours—to run scared and climb down defeated or leap out and believe. Suppose that each of us has a bell to ring and a Promised Land to enter, with nothing in the way but fear.

Death Standing Up

Birth is a beginning and death a destination.
And life is a journey.

RABBI ALVIN FINE

E ach summer of my childhood, we flew to a fishing lodge in Canada, our floatplane swooping down onto an expanse of water as huge as the sky. Just the three of us—my dad, my brother, and me. The lake water was so pure that all we had to do was dip a cup in and drink when we were thirsty. Eagles and hawks filled the sky, moose and bear the shoreline. The nearest dirt road was three hundred miles away and open only in the summer for logging trucks. Moss covered the jagged rocks jutting out of the gray-blue water.

We spent the days fishing. When the fish didn't bite, with a pull of the ripcord on our outboard motor, we skimmed across the lake in search of better luck. These boat rides could take thirty or forty minutes. Some fishermen at the lodge preferred to ride facing backward to avoid getting windburned or splashed. I liked to face the wind and the water head-on, so clean and cold it was like breathing snow.

As we sped along the water one morning, our boat a tiny speck in the vast sun-dappled world of water and stone, my father leaned over to our guide and shouted for him to stop. The boat fell silent as we glided to a gentle halt in the middle of the lake.

"It's your grandmother's *yahrtzeit* today," he said to my brother and me. Then the three of us said Kaddish together as the boat rocked softly beneath an unblemished sky. Three voices praising God's name in the wilderness. Three voices ascending to heaven. Our guide, an old Ojibwa Indian, looked on in silence. He seemed to recognize that what we were doing was important to our family and our tribe.

"That's the whole story right there," my dad said as we finished praying. Then he circled his finger in the air, signaling our guide to pull the ripcord and move on.

I had said Kaddish for my grandmother a few times before and have said it dozens of times since, but this time was different. On the lake I felt both small and great, closer to my father and brother, connected to the earth and the sky—alone, but part of something. It was the same combination of feelings I think the ancient rabbis hoped to create in us when they chose for us to memorialize our dead with a prayer that speaks only of life; a prayer that, by the way, must always be said standing. In the midst of sadness, when we least feel like it, the rabbis command us to stand up for life.

It's a lot like facing the wind and the water head-on, slowing down gently to recognize our losses—growing closer to the people we love—then pulling the ripcord and speeding off again full of hope for the future. As my dad likes to say, "That's the whole story right there."

CHAPTER 2

God

The race is not to the swift.

ECCLESIASTES

"YOU CAN'T PUT ONE TUCHUS IN TWO CHAIRS" is my father's not-so-quaint way of summing up the paradox of modern life. It's hard to be busy and balanced at the same time. It's hard to find the sacred in the everyday when the everyday is a blur.

I've confronted a lot of joy and sadness as a rabbi. Weddings, babies, miraculous recoveries, hugs from children, tears of joy—there's plenty of the good stuff to go around. But so, too, open wounds in the hospital, brain tumors in young fathers, divorce, murdered children—you name it. The problem is staying connected to it all. I can go from a wedding to a funeral to a bris in one day without thinking very much about it. It's not that I'm insensitive—just busy. I'm no different from most people—rabbis, salesclerks, attorneys, bus drivers, doctors, tailors, teachers, and parents—we all face a lot, but it's not very often that we face ourselves. Most of us are too busy living to really be alive. There was, however, that one afternoon the week before Rosh Hashanah nine years ago at the mikvah. The mikvah in my town is tended by a woman named Lillian, affectionately known among the local rabbis as "the mikvah lady." Since high school, I knew that the mikvah was a ritual bath used for conversions, by traditional Jewish women after menstruation, by other Jews for *kashering* dishes, and occasionally prior to a wedding, Shabbat, or the High Holy Days, but I had never actually been in one before. After witnessing the impact it had on a young woman I had just converted, I was curious. Looking at Lillian, I asked timidly, "Could I use the mikvah?"

Lillian hangs around a lot of rabbis, and she's seen the power of the mikvah at work in many people's lives. "Of course," she said warmly. "Go in, and take your time, Rabbi."

"Take your time," I thought to myself. "How many of us ever get to take our time at anything we do?"

I showered, brushed my teeth, trimmed my nails—the law requires that nothing come between me and the water that would surround me. Then, naked and alone, I entered the square, silent, blue-tiled chamber—built to Talmudic specifications—to immerse myself three times and recite three blessings. Descending the seven steps—one for each day of Creation—standing shoulder-high in the water, I gently lowered my head and pulled my knees to my chest. Floating in the warmth, I felt linked to generations of men and women who also sought refuge, sought God, sought themselves, in the mikvah. Suspended in the liquid silence, I was suspended, too, in an eternal, infinite moment. To my dismay, I sighed a sigh of sorrow. A sigh for all of the unfinished business in my life: for my grandfather, whom I had not seen in thirty years—still alive but cut off from me in some twisted family warfare I vaguely recall but do not understand. A sigh for my wife's cancer. Will it return? A sigh for my brother, my little brother whom I could not protect from the harshness of the world. A sigh for my lost loves—where are they now? Where am I now?

A sigh because I should be better, do more, study more, give more, write more, read more. What kind of father am I? My children, so beautiful, so pure. My wife's brilliant eyes, her strength and grace. My blessings. Distinct and separate images awakened all at once; psychic baggage never unpacked, moments pushed deep into the background were magically released to the untelling, all-knowing waters; to God.

The week before Rosh Hashanah 5748, I left that small, quiet place slowly, having uttered my High Holy Day prayers for the very first time in piety and truth. I left ready for redemption. Now I go back each year, curling like an embryo beneath the still water, making peace with my longings, counting my blessings, reminding myself of Lillian's advice: "Take your time, Rabbi. Take your time."

This is a chapter about embracing our ancestors and each other; discovering the everyday sacred within and around us, just by taking our time.

Roughhouse Weinbach

God is in this place, and I did not know it.

JACOB (GENESIS 28:16)

The place is anyplace where God lets down His ladder. And there is no way to determine where it may be but by being ready for it always.

JOHN RUSKIN

For years, one Sunday morning each month, I got on a bus with a group of twelve-year-olds to visit a convalescent hospital near the temple. There were nine Jewish residents among the dozens of patients who lay in small, plain rooms off dark hallways reeking from the smell of the aged and the sick. On our very first visit, the nursing staff wheeled the five Jewish patients who could get out of bed into the activity room to visit with the students and me. These five Jews were among the loneliest, least-cared-about Jews in Los Angeles. One of them told us we were her first visitors in ten years.

Four of the five seemed able enough to converse with the students and participate in the mock Shabbat service we planned for them. But one of the patients wheeled into the room seemed cut off from life. He sat slack-jawed and drooling, strapped into a wheelchair with his dull, clouded eyes rolled back into their sockets. Blind and listless he sat, oblivious to our presence. Everyone stayed far away from this hopeless stroke victim strapped into his chair.

Suddenly an elderly woman walked into the room, kissed him on the forehead and said, "Ben, it's Dorothy."

Slowly assimilating each syllable and then formulating a response somewhere deep in his stroke-damaged brain, Ben uttered a drawling reply, "Dor-ah-thee, let-me-lay-down."

The students and I stared in disbelief.

"No, Ben, you haven't had your lunch yet," Dorothy answered as she wiped his mouth and ran her hands lovingly through his hair.

Dorothy was Ben's sister. She had visited him every day since his stroke three years ago. Surprisingly, Ben could hear everything and even respond to simple questions if given long enough to absorb the words and think of an answer. What followed was a remarkable exchange.

I managed to explain to Ben who we were and why we were visiting. "Ben, what's your favorite Jewish food?" I asked.

"Chic-ken-soup" came the reply. And then almost thirty seconds later: "With mat-zah-balls-and-krep-lach."

"What's your favorite holiday?" asked one of the kids.

"Cha-nu-kah," he answered.

"Ask him about sports," Dorothy encouraged the kids.

Within a few minutes, Ben informed them that the Yankees were his favorite team and Yogi Berra his favorite catcher. We eventually learned that Ben used to be one of the few Jews on the professional wrestling circuit in the 1930s.

"Tell the kids your wrestling name, Ben," Dorothy prompted.

"Rough-house Wein-bach," Ben replied to a roar of laughter and approval from the fifteen students now totally captivated by breaking through what seemed an impenetrable barrier.

"There's never anyone to talk to him here," Dorothy explained. "All he ever wants to do is sleep. He almost never speaks."

Finally, it was time for our pretend Shabbat service. We lit the candles, recited the blessings, and sang "Shabbat Shalom." Suddenly, as if seeing a vision, Ben's expressionless face came alive, and he joined in the singing. "Shhh-aaaah-baaaht Shaaaaa-loh-ohmmmmm."

Somehow the melody reached him, shaking loose memories of Sabbaths long past. "He hasn't sung in three years," Dorothy said, fighting back tears.

There, in the most decrepit of places, a lost and lonely Jew sang out against the darkness and depression, against the cruelty and the ache. A Jew written off by us as impossible to reach, ignored like a leaf in the gutter...a miracle, waiting to be seen. There was God in you, Ben, and we didn't know.

Becoming a Blessing

Dead men don't praise God. The Torah was given to the living.

JACOB GLATSTEIN

Sherman, Texas, was a long way from the yeshivah. But that's where they told me my student pulpit was, so that's where I was going. Student pulpit duty is a rabbinical school requirement intended to help you learn the ropes by serving a weekend a month in a small community that can't support a full-time rabbi but still has enough life left in it to keep the synagogue doors open.

Congregation Beth Emet, with its twenty-five Jewish families hunkered down just south of the Oklahoma border, was my rabbinical boot camp. Other than the occasional High Holy Day when a retired rabbi from Dallas conducted services in the one-room synagogue, I was the first rabbi or student rabbi to visit Sherman on a regular basis since Jews arrived there in the early twentieth century. The notion of a rabbi was so new to the community that I was often referred to by non-Jews in town as "Rabbi Steven Leder, the pastor from the Hebrew church."

On my first visit, I pressed on doing all of the things an energetic, idealistic student rabbi was supposed to do: leading services, tutoring the few children, teaching adult education classes, visiting the Jewish businesses on Main Street, drinking iced tea with the temple president at the diner next to the pawnshop and the VFW post. Whenever I had some extra time on Saturday afternoon, I would visit the few elderly Jews in town who were too frail or sick to come to services on Friday night. Bill was one of those Jews.

Bill had a bad heart—so bad the doctors in Dallas told him he was best off at home, close to his oxygen and the telephone. His wife, Betti, was a practicing Baptist who had driven him to synagogue and had sat with him every High Holy Day for forty-five years. But now her eyes were bad, and even if Bill could go to synagogue, she couldn't drive him and be by his side.

It was my first visit to Bill and Betti's house. I imagined that I would chat a little about their lives, when they came to Sherman and why, maybe tell them a bit about myself, then wish them well and be on my way. At least, that's what I had planned as I stepped up onto the porch past the rusted chairs and knocked on the screen door.

The house looked as though it hadn't changed much inside for a long time, with its faded pictures, black-and-white TV, an ashtray from a cruise to Mexico in 1973. Bill was in the kitchen fixing us some iced tea and cutting the sponge cake Betti had made the night before. The three of us sat around the speckled Formica table, ate our white cake on orange plastic dishes, and chatted about this and that, just as I'd imagined it. Life seemed hard for them, yet neither seemed to mind too terribly much.

After an hour or so, my rabbinical duty done, I glanced at my watch, mentioned my next appointment, and stood up to leave. Just as I was thanking them and promising to visit again next month, Betti clutched my hand, quick and hard. "Perhaps you'd like to bless us, Rabbi," she said.

Bill, weak and awkward, nodded and whispered, "Yes. Bless us, Rabbi," as he held Betti's hand and reached for my own.

There we stood, grasping hands in that little Texas kitchen, in that little Texas town—the blind Baptist woman, the weak old Jew, and the bewildered rabbinical student who had only come for conversation. "A blessing?" I thought to myself, convinced that this was neither the time nor the place. "What am I supposed to say?"

But there they stood, eyes closed, hands held tight, fervent, expecting. And to my lips came the words of a three-thousand-year-old blessing spoken originally by the High Priest and used today by rabbis in sanctuaries of marble and glass: "May the Lord bless you and keep you." There in that Texas kitchen: "May the Lord illumine your life and be gracious unto you." Behind the tattered screen door: "May the Lord's spirit be upon you and grant you peace."

"Amen," said Bill and Betti as they opened their eyes, visibly moved. "Amen."

I've never forgotten that afternoon or that kitchen, because I learned an important lesson there. We can all bring blessings to people who need them. Blessings require no great sanctuary, no marble, no golden ark, no microphone. All a blessing takes—all seeing God takes—is a little time; a few words with two people locked in the silent struggles of life, seeking meaning and recognition amid their faded pictures. That's all it took, just a little time and a few kind words to say I wished them well and "God bless."

We could all manage that for the Bills and Bettis in our own lives; for everyone we meet and know caught up in the search for understanding and insight, craving notice and love. Such a simple thing, these blessings spoken or transmitted in a touch, a smile, a call; making of us blessings ourselves.

"Amen," said Bill and Betti as they opened their eyes. "Amen."

My Father's Fier Kashas

To give honor to your parents is even more important than honoring God.

JERUSALEM TALMUD

From the time I left home at seventeen until today, my father has called almost every week and asked me the same four questions. I have four siblings who are also queried in precisely the same way and with precisely the same frequency. By my count, that makes roughly five thousand times my dad has asked his children each of these questions:

1. "How's your car?"

2. "How's school?" (This later became "How's work?")

3. How are your finances?"

4. "Are you having any fun?" (This later became "How's your love life?")

He never asked, "How are you?" or "What's new?" He wanted details. Each question led to another and those to still more. Did I change the oil or wiper blades? Was I broke, or did I have enough money to have a little fun? Was my marriage holding up? Were we happy? Had I spoken to my siblings? When? What did they say?

We kids lovingly refer to this weekly inquisition as the *"Fier Kashas"*—a Yiddish reference to the four questions asked each year by the youngest child present at the Passover seder. Of course, at the seder, it's the children asking questions of the parents and the parents providing the answers. The other fifty-one weeks of the year, at least in my life, it's the other way around.

Lately, I find myself doing the same thing with my own children. I ask them a lot of questions—specific questions. What book did you read during story time? Why do you think the Cat in the Hat made such a mess? Do you make messes? What's the right thing to do when you make a mess? You learned about Martin Luther King, Jr., today; what do you think he was like? What do you think about the person who shot him? Why did you leave your bike out in the rain?

There's nothing novel or brilliant about parents asking kids questions. It's probably been going on since the first child left the cave to hunt and got back after curfew. What's novel, though, is what we do with questions at our seders. At seder, we openly encourage our children to ask us questions. We smile and laugh, applaud, hug and kiss them when, in the haggadah's ancient tongue, they ask us about the meaning of our traditions and our past. At the seder, the flow of life is reversed, with questions launched upstream from child to parent.

Oh, it's true that very young children often ask their parents a lot of questions. Sometimes they ask so many questions so repeatedly that we find ourselves begging them to stop. And then, somewhere just before adolescence sets in, they do stop. Once, while teaching a group of fifteen-year-old students, most of whom were estranged from their parents in typical but painful adolescent ways, I had them write down one question they would ask their parents if their parents had to answer them fully and truthfully. With slight variation but without exception, each student wanted to know the same thing. They wanted to know if their parents had been like them when they were fifteen. Did their parents ever have the same longings and fears? Did they make the same mistakes? Did they ever feel as alienated, as in love, chaotic and alive? Did Mom or Dad, in spite of the posturing and the nagging, really understand?

When I asked the kids why they never shared these sorts of questions with their parents, they shook their heads and replied, "They'll never tell us the truth." Maybe my students were exaggerating. But I got the feeling that once their questions turn from childlike to tough, a lot of us give kids the message that we'll do the asking and they'll do the answering, thank-you-very-much.

The seder suggests a different way: a night on which we applaud and uplift our children's questions, on which we hug, kiss, and answer them without fear. After the seder this year, it occurred to me that I ought to use the seder's model more than two nights a year. If it worked during Passover, why not during the rest of the year too? So now I take the time more often to ask my father the same four questions he's asked me every week of my adult life for over twenty years. After all, doesn't he have a car, work, money, and a marriage to worry about?

Questions were my father's way of learning and caring about me, but they have also become a way for me to learn and care about him. What began as annual questions about Passover while gathered around the seder table have become regular questions about my dad's life, gathering us closer than we have ever been before.

Dining with God

*It's not a bad thing to learn at the age of six that
you can't have every candy bar in the candy store.*

DENNIS PRAGER

Ever since I was a little boy unpacking my matzah sandwich in the school lunchroom, Passover has made me feel
different. Every year since then, the dietary restrictions of
Passover have accomplished their goal. Those who take the
prohibition against eating *chametz* (leaven) seriously find
their Jewish consciousness raised, feeling more keenly the
history of our ancestors and an affinity for our differences
from the Christian culture that surrounds us. But after
Passover, when the last matzah crumbs are gone, and the
uneaten macaroons are exiled to the back of the pantry or
the trash, we can't wait to get some rice, pasta, bread, cereal,
and cookies back into the house. We gorge ourselves on a
first meal of pizza or Kung Pao chicken and all is well on the
culinary front.

Not so fast. Guess what almost the entire Torah portion is
about for the week immediately following Passover—things we
can't eat. If it were just roadkill, mice, and lizards that were off
the kosher menu, things would be easy. But the Torah forbids a
lot of the good stuff too. Shrimp—out. Barbecued spare ribs—
uh, uh, uh. A nice fettuccine tossed with scallops in a lobster
cream sauce—no can do. Just when we think our freedom to eat
has returned, the Torah reminds us otherwise.

There have been many reasons offered for keeping kosher.
Some rabbinic authorities and physicians think it's healthier.
Other scholars are convinced that kashrut differentiates us
from non-Jews and prevents assimilation. Still others believe
that the Torah was attempting to wean us away from pagan-

ism by forbidding us to eat foods associated with it. There are those convinced that kashrut encourages more compassionate behavior toward our fellow creatures. And, of course, there are those who simply say, "It's God's will."

I wasn't always a rabbi, and I didn't always keep kosher. I grew up with a sort of schizophrenic sense of kashrut. For instance, we could never cook pork in the house, but it was okay to order in and eat on paper plates in the kitchen. Shellfish and cheeseburgers were in, but lard was out. Stone crabs, yes; catfish, no. Go figure.

As I grew, studying and caring more about Jewish observance, I began to experiment with not eating pork and shellfish, while at the same time avoiding meat and dairy at the same meal. Kashrut, once viewed by me as inconsistent at best and nonsense at worst, suddenly began to matter. Sure, I miss pepperoni pizza and shrimp. Yeah, I'd like to top off my burger and onion rings with a hot fudge sundae for dessert. But I don't.

Do I feel healthier? Sometimes. But anyone who's ever ordered a nice, fatty piece of brisket on a kaiser roll au jus with a side of fries knows that kosher food can be as bad for you as nonkosher food. Does keeping kosher make me feel different from non-Jews? You bet. Have I avoided paganism? So far. Am I more compassionate? I think so. Is it God's will? I'm not sure, but my ancestors thought so, and sometimes that's good enough. This much I know for certain. That feeling I had in my elementary school lunchroom of being special every time I pulled my matzah sandwich and macaroons out of my brown paper bag is a feeling I used to have only one week a year. Now, as an adult who has grown into kashrut at his own pace and in his own way, I have that feeling of uniqueness and connection at every meal.

Passover always comes to an end. The matzah crumbs are dust-busted away, but not the opportunity to express something holy in how and what we eat. For Jews, the table can be a sacred place to dine with God more than one week a year. Besides, to shellfish, you could be allergic....

God Bless You, Young Man

The question of bread for myself is a material question, but the question of bread for my neighbor is a spiritual question.

NIKOLAI BERDAYEV

M y son, Aaron, has a personal net worth of about sixty-five dollars (excluding monthly contributions made by his parents to a college fund). He's an enterprising kid who picks up a dollar here and a dollar there by watering our neighbors' plants when they're out of town, sweeping the kitchen floor, helping me clean out the gutters, and hitting up his grandparents whenever possible. All of his paper money is stored in his blue plastic wallet from Disneyland; the change is deposited in one of those battery-operated banks that sorts it into stacks. There aren't many things Aaron loves more than putting a full stack into a paper wrapper and hiding it in his closet.

A few weeks ago, when Aaron decided to spend some of his own money on a foam-dart-propelling piece of plastic shaped like a stingray, I gave the okay along with the news that it was time to give some of his money away to the homeless. He didn't understand. At the risk of sounding like a rabbi to my own son, I nevertheless explained that the Torah says we have to give some of our money away to people who have less. The negotiation began.

"Why can't we give some of your money?" he asked.

"I do. But that's my money," I countered. "You have to give some of yours."

When Aaron realized there was no getting out of it, he started talking percentages. "How about this?" he said hopefully while pulling out a roll of pennies.

"Nope, not enough," I told him as I withdrew six dollars and fifty cents in change from behind the T-shirts. "This is how much the Torah says you should give."

After agreeing to the $6.50, Aaron tried to put the best spin possible on the deal by remarking, "Besides, I can always make more money."

Next we had to decide on a distribution strategy. Normally I'm a believer in giving to programs that take a systemic approach to fighting poverty and homelessness. But dealing with a child sometimes requires a more visceral experience. So off we went to give the money directly to someone who needed it. Aaron suggested the homeless man who camps out in front of our local coffee shop.

Aaron approached him cautiously—not because he was afraid but because he's generally shy. He handed the man the money and merely said, "Here. This is for you."

The man, wrapped in dirty layers, smooth, dark skin and bright brown eyes, both young and old, friendly and frightening, smiled as he reached out for the money and bent down to shake Aaron's hand. "God bless you, young man" were the words he chose to recognize Aaron's gesture.

"Bye," said Aaron, as we walked quietly back to the car.

In a way, what I was trying to teach Aaron was what the Torah intended all of us to learn when it designated the sabbatical and jubilee years—fixed times when debts were forgiven, and property lost through bankruptcy and misfortune was returned to its original owner. This was our uniquely Jewish way of trying to prevent multi-generational poverty. There is also talk about tithing in the Torah—giving ten percent of what you have in order to help the needy. All of these rules are spoken against the background of a simple, truthful verse in which God says, "The land is Mine; you are but strangers and residents."

It's the Torah's way of reminding us that what we have didn't really come from us. Our accomplishments are a result of God-given talents, resources, and good fortune that ultimately must be shared with others. Recognizing that we didn't get to where we are all by ourselves is not only humbling, it's an uplifting, spiritual recognition of God. As the Torah puts it, when we give back, God will be "ever present in your midst."

The Torah and that homeless man in front of the coffee shop had it right: We find God by giving. So, to Aaron and to all those children like him who must learn to give and whose parents must teach them, "God bless you."

Nothing Much

Who is rich? The one who is happy with what he has.

PIRKE AVOT

"Nothing" is a word I used a lot recently. It was my thirty-seventh birthday, and people wanted to know what my plans were for the big day. Everyone got the same answer: "Nothing much."

It was true: I really didn't do anything all that special on my birthday. Aaron and I get up early to play street hockey in front of the house. He pretends he's Wayne Gretzky; I try to stop the puck. Somehow he always manages a goal and then shouts, "Gretzky scores!" throwing his little arms in the air and hugging me, just like the real players on TV. Later, out come Betsy and our beautiful, redheaded, five-year-old Hannah; twirling in her dress, she greets me, ballerina-like and smiling.

In we go to the den, where I'm greeted with a stack of presents. A shirt, a tie, a pair of gardening gloves, and finally, a grape lollipop taken from Aaron's private stash and handed to me with the words "Happy birthday, Daddy. I love you."

Next, shower time. Aaron asks if he can rinse the shampoo out of my hair with his super-soaker squirt gun. I agree. Finally, it's off to the shopping center to exchange the shirt for a larger one (an annual rite of passage for many men my age), some pizza, and back home for naps.

Don't get me wrong; we did have some big plans for my birthday. But after putting the kids to sleep, Betsy and I looked at each other and knew we were just too tired to go out. We canceled the babysitter. I defrosted some macaroni and cheese in the microwave; Betsy had a bagel. We watched a little TV and then fell asleep holding hands under the covers. The gentle end of an ordinary day.

The next day I was back to putting on a suit and doing what rabbis do—the everyday stuff. Except for some of the phone calls.

One of our young congregants reaches me early—she just lost her job. She is worried about losing her apartment and having no place to live. "Do you know anyone who can help me?" she asks.

David calls. "Rabbi," his voice trembles through his tears, "yesterday my wife told me she's leaving. What's going to happen to our twenty-month-old son, to me, to my life? Will you talk to her, Rabbi, please?"

After years of infertility treatments, Donna is finally pregnant and wants to say thank-you for the counseling I'd done with her.

I suppose we all get tired of our routine lives now and then. We all yearn for some big days with big plans. But we take a lot for granted too. How well my phone calls reminded me.

How desperately each of those I talked to, and so many others in this unkind world, hunger for the simple pleasures of work, family, and human love, of backyard hockey games and hugs, macaroni and cheese, twirling ballerinas, and a hand to hold under the covers of a gentle, ordinary day.

Thank God for days filled with nothing much at all. Nothing much is more than enough.

Life Is a Desert

Every brush with death is a brush with life.

RABBI LAWRENCE KUSHNER

B arbara was beautiful—sparkling eyes and thick, wavy brown hair. Barbara was sweet and funny. Barbara was moral and strong. Barbara is gone.

After a fierce war with cancer, including marrow harvesting, six weeks near death on a respirator in the ICU with lung, kidney, and heart failure, bloating, wasting, death vigils, despair, glimmers of life, tiny recoveries with the chance for a few good months that in three days turned to coma and death—she's gone.

Her husband, her three teenage children, the hundreds, even thousands of lives she touched, ache for her smile and walk with heavy hearts through the surreal world of eulogies, clods of earth thunking on a casket that houses her body but never her soul, white limousines with blackened windows protecting the most shattered mourners returning home for shiva.

I ask the same questions everyone asks after a tragedy. What if it were me, my wife, my kids? And then, knowing how grateful I am, I perform a personal ritual upon departing the cemetery. Some days I can only leave a message. Today Betsy is home.

"Honey, it's me," I say over the crackle of the car phone.

"Is it over?" she asks.

"Yeah," I answer. "You know I love you."

"I love you too."

Without having to say it, we both know why I call. We understand this ritual. It's a simple recognition that we have everything we need because we have our children and each other.

Back at Barbara's house—it will always feel like Barbara's house—we wash our hands, trying to leave death outside. We eat, we look for some way to help, something to say, and then we pray. All of us, a hundred-strong, stand together praising God even in the face of suffering. Barbara's kids smile at me, knowing I am proud they can chant along; their Judaism has helped them. Arm in arm, the room knit together by a family's pain, we sing "Oseh Shalom," begging for peace and comfort, finding it in each other.

You might suppose that the death of a young woman, a life force so determined and true, would leave in its path only faithless cynicism and doubt. You might expect anger and rejection, an accusatory finger pointed at God. But that's not what most of us felt saying goodbye to Barbara with our arms around each other. We listened to story after story about how she made life better in her neighborhood, her kids' schools, her home, her marriage, and her friendships. We felt the worth and the power of life, both hers and ours. We counted our blessings of family and love.

There is an entire book of the Torah called *Bamidbar*—In the Wilderness. It's the story of our ancestors' wanderings in the harsh desert, the painful failures and losses that transformed us from slaves into chosen people ready to enter a holy land. Jews first found God in the desert. The Torah is revealed in the desert. Most of the Hebrew prophets lived in the desert. The desert is hard and empty; it makes you appreciate the most fundamental things—shade, water, the presence of another human being. At times, like hospital visits and funerals, life, too, is hard and empty, teaching its own lessons about what's important, creating its own encounter with the Divine.

God is in the desert for the same reason God is in sorrow and death. Each one strips away the insignificant and the petty, showing us tougher, deeper, better truths; bringing us closer to God by bringing us closer to each other, ever more grateful for our lives and our blessings.

CHAPTER 3

*I have believed in money, but all I got
was greed.*

*I have believed in vengeance, but all I did
was bleed.*

*I have believed in fame, but fame turned its
back on me.*

*If I had only believed in love, I would have
been set free.*

PETER HIMMELMAN

A MAN ONCE STOOD BEFORE GOD, his heart breaking from the pain and injustice in the world. "Dear God," he cried out, "look at all the suffering, the anguish and distress in Your world. Why don't You send help?"

God responded, "I did send help. I sent you."

I believe we are sent by God to conquer evil, soothe suffering, and create joy. When we reach out to people in pain, we do God's work. Why there needs to be pain and suffering in the first place is an understandable question but ultimately a pointless one. There are those who believe suffering is inflicted by God as punishment for sin. Others simply accept on faith that what seems like evil to us actually has a purpose in God's great plan, but being human means we can never fully appreciate its role. Then there are those who refuse to blame God for evil; they blame humanity instead. I am one of those. For me, for most of us, I suspect, God is not an omnipotent, supernatural power but a power manifest in humanity at its best. If this is so, then the answer to cruelty lies not in heaven but on earth. Salvation will come to us not from God above but from each other.

That's the lesson of an old story about a small, charming village in the Polish countryside where the villagers consulted the rabbi in all matters large and small. So it was with great joy that they looked forward to the marriage of the rabbi's only son. In just two weeks, the fine young man would stand beneath the chuppah with the tailor's beautiful daughter.

In order to guarantee a truly joyous wedding, the mayor instructed Mendel the Carpenter to construct a barrel the size of a small water tower in the middle of the town square. So high was it that one had to use a ladder to reach the top. When the barrel was finished, the mayor decreed that each villager had two weeks to bring a bucket full of the best wine from his cellar to the town square and empty it into the tall barrel. On the evening of the wedding, the barrel would be tapped, and from it would flow the sweetest wine the town had ever known. Everyone could drink his fill, sing, dance, and praise God for the love of bride and groom.

Every day for two weeks, there was a steady stream of villagers walking to the town square with pails in hand. Each one climbed the ladder to the very top, lifted the pail over his or her head, and poured its contents into the massive barrel.

Finally, the much-awaited evening arrived. During the ceremony, there were tears of joy for the beloved rabbi and for the beautiful bride and worthy groom now joined together for life. Soon after, the mayor decided the time had come to tap the barrel, enjoy the luscious red wine gathered bucket by bucket during the past weeks, and celebrate as the town had never celebrated before.

As the mayor approached the barrel with a tap and mallet, the villagers crowded around him, grasping empty mugs in their eager hands. With a smile as wide as all of Poland, he climbed the ladder, pounded in the tap, and placed his hand on the spigot, ready to unleash a torrent of wine. *"Mazal tov,* and praised be God for this wonderful day in the history of our village and of our people,"* the mayor exclaimed as he turned the spigot and waited for his mug to fill.

Suddenly the entire village fell silent, as silent as death itself. For, when the mayor turned the spigot, out of it flowed nothing but water. Looking into each other's eyes, the villagers knew exactly what had happened. Throughout the past weeks, each supposed that they could get by with adding water instead of wine to the barrel, while everyone else did their fair share.

After all, what difference would one pail of water make in all of that wine?

After standing silently in the square for what seemed like hours, they returned to their own homes filled with shame and despair. It was the saddest wedding celebration the town had ever known.

It's an old story, but were the choices then really any different than they are today? We all have to decide what we want, what kind of Judaism, and what kind of world we will create for ourselves and our children. Do we want a diluted, minimalist faith in a selfish world, or do we want to drink deep from the rich sweetness of our tradition? Do we want to be known as Jews who take their exercise routine more seriously than their Judaism and their obligations to society, or as a people that uplifts itself and others with learning, goodness, and prayer? Will we accept, or leave to others, the responsibilities and the joys of being a Jew and doing God's work?

The Cure for Cruelty

All I ever cared about was that you be a mensch.

LEONARD LEDER

Mensch—a concept virtually every Jew understands but can't explain. Leo Rosten came close in his book *The Joys of Yiddish*. Under the entry *Mensch* he writes:

"As a child, I often heard it said that the finest thing you can say about a person is that he is a *mensch*. To be a mensch has nothing to do with success, wealth or status. A judge can be a *zhlob*, a millionaire can be a *momzer*; a professor a *schlemiel*. The key to being 'a real mensch' is ... character. Many a poor man, many an ignorant man, is a mensch."

It's hard to define a mensch. In fact, it's easier to say what a mensch is not than to say what a mensch is. Take, for instance, the joke about Goldstein, an accountant who does some financial work for the mob.

When an Argentinean robber, also working for the mob, absconds with $250,000 stolen from a bank, the mob sends an enforcer along with the Spanish-speaking Goldstein to find the robber. They catch up with him in Buenos Aires.

"Ask him where the money is," the enforcer tells Goldstein.

Goldstein asks the man. The bank robber says, "I won't tell you a thing."

Goldstein translates what the Argentinean has said. The enforcer shoots the man in his right knee.

"Ask him again," the enforcer says.

Again the man says, "I won't tell. I'm never going to tell."

The enforcer shoots him in the other knee.

"Tell him," the enforcer says, "that the next shot goes right through his head."

Goldstein translates the enforcer's words.

The Argentinean says, "Tell him it's in the trunk of my car, under the spare tire."

Goldstein turns to the enforcer. "He says he's not afraid to die."

Needless to say, Goldstein is not a mensch. Yes, it's easy enough to say what a mensch is not. To define what a mensch is, well, that's a far more difficult task. But since mensches are the cure for the world's troubles, I offer now my own humble attempt at a definition and an approach. You can call it "Rabbi Leder's Eleven Suggestions for Becoming a Mensch."

1. Remember what success really means. As Rabbi Neil Kurshan points out: "The Talmud states that when a child is born, it is visited by an angel who requires that the child take a simple oath: 'Be righteous, and never be wicked.' A child is not asked to be brilliant, cute, athletic, or popular. A child is asked to become kind, honest, understanding."

    A mensch worries more about being better than about being better off.

2. Do we tell our children to be honest but sneak them into the movies for the under-twelve price when they're twelve and a half? Do we tell them we're going out to a meeting, and they later find out we went to dinner and a movie? Do we tell them to be lawful and then park in the handicapped spot? Do we tell our kids to be kind to their brothers and sisters, while we haven't spoken to our own siblings in months? Do our children hear us say we care about the poor and then watch us ignore their outstretched hands and their hungry eyes as we walk by them in our Armani and our Chanel?

    A mensch is always a mensch, in word and in deed.

3. A mensch treats everyone decently. When a man who served as the White House stenographer for over forty years retired, he was asked which president he enjoyed working for the most. He answered that Harry Truman was his favorite because he was the only president who called him by his name.

    A mensch doesn't treat anyone like hired help— even hired help.

4. When a friend is sick, experiences a divorce, tragedy, or death in the family, no matter how busy, a mensch takes the time to call or visit. A mensch reaches out to people who ache instead of running away.

    A mensch doesn't disappear.

5. Do the people closest to us see us angrier about rush hour traffic and the housekeeper folding our laundry improperly than we are over racism, pollution, or violence?

    A mensch knows the difference between real problems and minor annoyances.

6. One of the most famous sayings in all of Judaism is by Rabbi Hillel in the Talmud: "If I am not for myself, who will be for me? And if I am only for myself, what am I? And if not now, when?" This was Hillel's plea for a life balanced between personal and communal obligations, appreciating the urgency of both.

    A mensch gives more money to charity than he or she can afford and more time to the community than he or she has to spare, but somehow always manages to be home when needed.

7. Maybe we don't use the "N" word in our homes. But what words do we use—fag, dyke, bitch, schvartze, goy? Whoever said, "sticks and stones may break my bones, but words will never hurt me," was wrong.

   We can wound with words; a mensch is careful not to.

8. Black, white, brown, or some combination; man or woman; young or old; married or single; thin or overweight; straight or gay—a mensch really doesn't care.

   The only thing that matters to a mensch is whether you, too, are a mensch.

9. Do you cheat in sports or in business? Have you ever seen your child cheating at something—even just a little bit—and done nothing about it?

   A mensch is honest—always.

10. A mensch doesn't gossip.

11. A therapist once said that ninety percent of what she treats people for could have been prevented or cured by ordinary kindness. A kind word, a call, a touch—the world is starving for kindness.

    A mensch is kind.

Everyone wants the world to be a better place. Being a mensch is the best way to make it happen.

Penny and Duane

Poverty is the most terrible of all sufferings.

EXODUS RABBAH

My elementary school in St. Louis Park, Minnesota, was like most suburban elementary schools: It was in the Midwest, in the mid-sixties, full of middle-class kids. Although a few kids were from wealthier or poorer families than most, the beauty of the place and the time was that we never really knew the difference. Until one seemingly ordinary fall day.

Penny, who had moved into town a few months earlier from Virginia, always seemed a little quiet and withdrawn. She was the only new kid in the class and the only one in the entire school with a Southern accent. We used to tease her about it sometimes. Penny wore drab clothes and fell asleep a lot in class, but for the most part, no one seemed to pay her much mind. Until it was her day for show-and-tell.

Penny didn't have anything to show, but she did have something to tell. In a voice that was even, controlled, and filled with resignation, she stood up and told the class: "My family has no money 'cuz my daddy lost his job drivin' a truck; that's why I'm wearin' this old dress." She was ten years old.

Most of us were dumbstruck—we were the children of professionals and small business owners. Our fathers all had steady jobs, and we lived in nice neighborhoods. We didn't know anyone who was poor...or so we thought.

After Penny finished she just stood there, a little hunched and pale, silent, alone. The quiet lasted a long time.

"My dad owns a company that uses truck drivers. Maybe he can help," offered Duane Hamilton. It was such a simple, innocent, decent moment.

"Well, that's very nice, Duane," said Miss Gibbons. "Let's see if we can get your two fathers together."

Somehow, we all felt better, and the day moved on. But I've never forgotten Penny and Duane; interestingly enough, neither has the Torah. I say neither has the Torah because Torah gives us the antidote to poverty: it's called the *yovel* or jubilee year.

The jubilee year required that every fifty years, all property revert to its original owners. According to the tradition, after the conquest of Canaan, each family received an equal share of land provided to them by God. At least in theory, at one point in Israelite history, each family had an equal slice of the prosperity pie. The jubilee year ensured that everyone who had suffered financial loss got their original piece of the pie back after fifty years. The jubilee year also required that all debts be nullified and all slaves be set free. Theoretically, then, no one could remain very poor, or very rich, for very long.

Scholars doubt whether the jubilee year was ever actually practiced in ancient Israel, and the chasm then between rich and poor was as wide, if not wider than, it is today. But whether or not it actually was observed, the jubilee year represents an important Jewish ideal: No one should be allowed to languish in poverty for long. The jubilee was the Torah's plea for a periodic redistribution of wealth in order to prevent the shame of a permanent underclass.

All of this might seem like a lot of biblical nonsense to some. But the idea of redistribution of wealth, the idea of climbing out of poverty with the help of others, the idea of a fair fight in the economic struggle for survival, should be no laughing matter to Jews.

We all know how dangerous and wrong it is for any city or society to allow a permanent underclass to struggle through grinding poverty from generation to generation. We all know the kind of despair, upheaval, and rioting a cycle of unceasing poverty can bring. The simple truth is that we cannot expect to keep what we have if we aren't willing to share with those who have less.

It's been many years since that Midwestern, middle-class school in the mid-sixties. I have no idea what became of Penny, but I do know that I'll never forget her—the Torah won't allow it.

Wise Up

Expecting the world to treat you fairly because you are a good person is like expecting the bull not to charge you because you are a vegetarian.

RABBI HAROLD KUSHNER

One thing's for sure—Judaism is a practical religion. When the Torah wanted to remind us of our wandering in the desert, humble beginnings, and precarious place among the nations, instead of opting for myth, metaphor, or prayer, it demanded the real thing—a week of sleeping and eating in a rickety booth. For anyone who's ever taken Sukkot seriously, the Torah's wisdom is abundantly clear. For anyone who hasn't, take my word for it—a week in a sukkah adds up to a pretty good lesson in humility.

Sure, the first day is kind of exciting. We get to build and decorate the whole thing with fresh green palm branches, gourds, and fruit. If we're lucky, there's a gentle Santa Ana breeze to keep us warm while we dine with our family and then drift gently off to sleep. But what about those Jews in Minnesota, Toronto, and Odessa freezing their behinds off just to observe the mitzvah of dwelling in the sukkah?

Sukkot can get a little rough, even for those of us lucky enough to live in warm places like Southern California. After about three days, that balmy weather starts to rot the fruit and gourds. We curse the thought of trying to get a good night's sleep on one of those stupid inflatable mattresses. Then, just when our aching backs can take no more, we get soaked, either by rain or, if you're like me, by the automatic sprinklers you forgot to turn off. Some holiday, huh?

There's actually a fair amount of thought given by the rabbis to the hardships of Sukkot, especially the eventuality of rain. According to the Talmud, if it's raining so hard that it spoils your porridge, it's permissible to leave the sukkah and finish your meal in the house. The same is true for sleeping. If it's raining too hard, you can snuggle up in your real bed until morning. These seem like reasonable enough accommodations to Mother Nature. But, for me, the real question isn't when we can leave the sukkah if it's raining, but why it sometimes rains at all. If we think about it, the idea of rain during Sukkot makes no sense. Why would God command us to eat and sleep in the sukkah and at the same time make that commandment impossible to fulfill by causing it to rain?

There are a lot of possible answers to this dilemma. Maybe God doesn't control when it rains in the first place. Maybe God does control the rainfall, and a downpour during Sukkot is a sign of God's displeasure with the Jewish people. Maybe there is no God, Sukkot was invented by human beings, and rain during the holiday means nothing at all. Any of these are possible, but I prefer the Talmud's own explanation. "To what can rain during Sukkot be compared?" the sages ask. "To a servant [a righteous person] who comes to fill his master's [God's] cup, and the master throws the water back into his face."

For the ancient rabbis, rain during Sukkot was a reminder that we can do everything right and still suffer tragedy. Like the rabbi I knew who worked out, lifted weights, and ran on the treadmill almost every day but still had a heart attack in his mid-forties—he died at the gym. What about Eric, my religiously devout gardener, who works in the hot sun more hours a week and harder than a professional athlete but makes less than one-thousandth the money? What about Syd, the seventy-one-year-old philanthropist and mensch who gave time and money to Los Angeles and its Jewish community —stricken with leukemia and gone within a month?

Rain on Sukkot, my rabbi friend, my gardener, and Syd, are all a lesson about goodness. If you think being good prevents anything bad from ever happening to you, wise up. Serving God and humanity guarantees meaning and purpose, not the lack of sorrow. No matter how good we are, sooner or later rain comes to our sukkah; no matter how well we serve God, once in a while we get hit in the face with cold water...and it all adds up to a pretty good lesson in humility.

God's Loneliest Creatures

The weakness of men is the facade of strength.

LAWRENCE DIGGS

Jewish tradition tried to teach a wonderful lesson about being a man. It was called the minyan, and when you turned thirteen, you were obligated to join one. I'm not an anthropologist, but I'll bet something similar exists in every culture. The minyan was simply a group of ten men who gathered every day in the early morning and late afternoon to pray. Often the prayers ended with a shot of booze for everyone involved.

Besides praying twice daily, the men of a minyan went to each other's weddings, welcomed each other's children into the world, and then watched those same children get married. They saw themselves age with stubble and paunch, then buried each other's loved ones and each other.

Imagine the potential of spending an hour every morning and afternoon with the same ten guys. Having a sense of obligation for other men, being involved in their lives, touching something spiritual and eternal with them—that's what the minyan could have been about. Instead, the men of the minyan usually remained spectators in each other's lives. They prayed each morning out of a sense of duty, had a drink, and went to work. They prayed each afternoon and went home. All of them, every day, in relative silence.

For most Jews today, minyans are gone—opportunities lost. It's considered passé, and by some people even immoral, to separate men and women. In fact, most of our all-male environments are gone. Don't get me wrong: organizations that excluded women and denied them the power they rightly deserve in society should be gone. But in the process, men lost the opportunity to create something they need and have always lacked—times and places to talk and to be with each other.

There are a few places left—topless bars and stadiums. But men don't really go to these places to be with other men in meaningful ways. We sit in bars and stadiums by the hundreds of thousands, week after week, watching but not talking...at least not about anything that matters. Men almost never talk to other men about feelings because it requires unlearning a lifetime of defensive and aggressive posturing—the silent sizing up of the other, the camouflaging of spirit and soul bequeathed to us by generations of men who went to work and went to war and didn't want to talk about it, thank-you-very-much.

Early on, most men learned a harsh, destructive lesson about manhood. A lot of the older men in our lives extolled the virtues of going it alone. Instead of learning how to reach out to other men as allies and friends, we somehow got the idea that they were competitors. Too many of us were taught by fathers, coaches, bosses, and superheroes that asking for help wasn't intelligent or strong but foolish and weak. For so many, to be a man means to talk around things and keep one's guard up, to carry the unique weight of manhood in mighty silence. Men are God's loneliest creatures.

Sure, we have friends: our racquetball partner, our poker buddies, our drinking buddies, our coworkers. But they're not like the deep, whole friendships that women seem to cultivate with ease. Our friendships with other men tend to be limited; intense in safe areas—sports or business or politics—and silent about most others. It's no wonder men are lost and misunderstood. How can we ever know each other, how can we ever be understood, in silence?

At my synagogue, we're struggling to create something the minyan could have provided if men were better at talking to each other. It's not exactly a product of the men's movement (few of us relish the thought of running through the woods singing cowboy songs and hugging other hairy men). We're on to something different.

Sixty of us, aged twenty-two to seventy-five, married, single, and divorced, meet every month for dinner and a discussion about a predetermined topic. We don't talk about sports, business, or politics. Instead, we are plunging into new, uncharted waters for most of us—we are sharing our stories.

At our first meeting, men who barely knew each other confronted what they learned from their fathers about being a man. Titles, status, age—none of it mattered, none of it separated us that night. We poured out our confusion, anger, sadness, love, and fear of our fathers. We talked about the ways, good and bad, that we resembled them. More desperately than any of us knew, we needed to tell our stories to other men we hoped would understand.

At our third meeting, we talked about our relationships with women. We said things we could never say with women in the room and yet things we had never shared with any man. Things about how painful and muddy our marriages sometimes become. About the sex we are not having. About the workaholism we inherited from our fathers. About the burnout we feel at home and at the office. We talked about growing old—the diabetes, the heart attacks, the prostate cancer. By forcing ourselves to confront the things all men experience but rarely discuss, we've achieved the greatest success of all. We are slowly beginning to share with each other, to understand each other, and be understood ourselves.

The meetings never end on time. Each of us tries to tell one more story, one last moment of connection—the minyan's potential realized. Men have never been very good at it, but we are learning to unbuckle our emotional armor. We tell our stories, and we tell the truth, revealing just how fragile and strong we are, reaching out to other men for help, becoming the minyan's rightful heirs; piercing the mighty silence of manhood, we are God's loneliest creatures no longer.

CHAPTER 4

Miracles

The whole cosmic order is one miracle. No room is left for single or exceptional miracles.

RABBI KAUFMAN KOHLER

AT THE CONCLUSION of a meeting with a group of twenty or so rabbis, one stood up and asked the rest of us to say a special prayer for the sick at our respective synagogues that evening. "Who was sick?" we wondered.

"My husband," she said. "He is dying."

"Don't say that," one of the Orthodox rabbis responded.

"Look," she said. "I have to be realistic. It'll be a miracle if he makes it more than the next few weeks."

"But miracles are real," retorted the other rabbi with passion. "You mustn't give up hope."

I've thought a lot about that brief exchange, about the rabbi's fervent plea on behalf of miracles. Most of us have heard of someone who made a remarkable medical recovery, narrowly escaped disaster, or won the lottery. But for me, these beating-the-odds miracles don't really demonstrate anything miraculous as much as they demonstrate the limits of our ability to predict the future.

For me, the truly miraculous experiences and individuals are those that regularly occur around us and yet transport us beyond our everyday lives; the extraordinary ordinary— transcendent encounters with powers ever-present in nature and in us. "I who am blind," wrote Helen Keller, "can give one hint to those who see.... Hear the music of voices, the song of a bird, the mighty strains of an orchestra.... Touch each object you want to touch.... Smell the perfume of flowers, taste with relish each morsel ... glory in all the facets of pleasure and beauty which the world reveals."

Sometimes miracles are minuscule things, a single cell dividing, the platelets in our blood, a walk. Other times, miracles come in larger sizes: sequoias or oceans. Most of all, there are the miracles we perform; life-giving, loving, courageous miracles that come from understanding our place and purpose in the world, that come from reaching out and reaching down to others. The miraculous is the common and the constant: birth, teaching, our breath. The miraculous is everywhere, though we sometimes fail to see it.

Pheresis

Blessed is our Eternal God, Creator of the universe, who has made our bodies with wisdom, combining veins, arteries and vital organs.

JEWISH PRAYER BOOK

I didn't know a thing about pheresis until Ethan called. At twenty-four years old, this record producer and frequent attender of the monthly study group for young professionals I held in my living room was worried about dying. Diagnosed with a brain tumor, having survived radical surgery, radiation, and chemo, he needed my help. Actually, he needed my platelets.

Platelets are the component in whole blood that helps control bleeding. About one tablespoon's worth can be collected from a unit of whole blood, and they can only be stored for about five days. Pheresis is the term for collecting platelets directly from a donor's blood. Leukemia, cancer, aplastic-anemia, and marrow-transplant patients all need platelets. Platelets also help stop bleeding in surgery. Platelets are precious. Platelets are life.

Ethan called me when chemotherapy had savaged his ability to produce platelets. His girlfriend had already given. Now he was in search of someone else who was safe and trustworthy (read: monogamous, nonintravenous-drug-using, stable, able-to-take-two-hours-off-in-the-middle-of-the-day sort of person). Who better than the rabbi?

"I need them today," Ethan said with a hint of desperation in his voice. "I called the hospital. They can take you at 2:00 P.M. Please?"

By 2:05 P.M., I was having my finger pricked and being asked a lot of questions about my sex life. "Did I ever receive money for sex?" the nurse wanted to know.

"I never even received a thank-you," I quipped in my best Groucho voice. She smiled politely. I guess she'd heard it all before.

By 2:30 P.M., the joking had stopped and the most amazing thing started. With me propped up on a comfortable bed and both arms extended, the nurse swabbed my bulging veins with betadine then deftly slid a needle into each with absolute precision. Clear, thin tubes ran from the needles in each arm into a whirring machine behind the bed. It was then that I realized that I was part of a complete cycle.

The machine drew a steady stream of blood from my right arm; spun it to remove the platelets; stored them in a thick, plastic bag; replaced the lost platelets with a saline solution; then pumped the saline and my blood (minus the harvested platelets) back into my left arm. For two hours, the machine and I were one—a closed circuit, an interdependent loop, give and take, flow and ebb. My lips tingled and my body chilled. The nurse laid two blankets on me. Warming, I settled into the quiet and the wait.

There were others giving too—platelets, plasma, blood. Some of them donated for no reason other than anonymous good. Most were there because it was one of the few tangible things they could do to help a loved one facing the scalpel or the oncologist. I imagined being there for my own freckle-faced boy or redheaded little girl, for my wife or my dad. What if one of them got cancer? What if I did? Those people next to me, their arms sprouting tubes of red, filling bags as they pumped and squeezed a foam ball—whose life were they here to save?

If you're ever feeling sorry for yourself, stop by this room. Marvel at the miracle of people giving a little of themselves and infusing it into someone they love. Be grateful for every day that someone isn't you.

"You're finished," the nurse told me as she bandaged the inside of my arm.

"Can I see it?" I asked as she unhooked the bag of platelets from behind me. There in her hands rested a little pouch of thick yellow fluid; miracle juice extracted from my blood and offered up to another.

The Torah tells us that "Anyone who eats blood will be cut off." In a total of five places, using more or less the same words, it repeats the prohibition, reminding us that "blood is life." Long before pheresis, our ancestors recognized and respected the miraculous power in blood. Today we can not only uplift and sanctify that power, we can transfuse it.

It's been a year now, and Ethan is doing fine. I saw him at shul for Purim. We just smiled at each other across the room. I will always be grateful to him for drawing me into the world of miracle-doers, selfless givers, and grateful receivers—teaching me what the Torah teaches and then some: that blood is life, and life is ours to give.

A Modern Maccabee

The little and pure is much.

BAHYA

True, he was born about twenty-one centuries too late to stand by Judah Maccabee's side in the bloody guerrilla war fought against the Assyrians and their Jewish followers who wanted to replace Judaism with the gymnasium and God with Zeus. True, he was ineligible for more recent battles— World War II or the Arab-Israeli wars—affecting the Jewish future, but make no mistake, my father was a Maccabee. Without ever having to fight in a war, my dad won a lot of important battles and, by the way, never more elegantly than in 1966 in Miami Beach.

Nineteen sixty-six marked the beginning of a long-standing December tradition, when my parents packed themselves up, along with their five children, and fled the Minnesota cold for two glorious, sun-baked weeks in Miami Beach, Florida. It was over thirty years ago, but I still remember feeling the thick, humid air hit me as I walked off the plane in what any Minnesotan in December would call a tropical paradise. I marveled at the sight of my first palm tree as we left the airport. It was nothing short of miraculous to me that we could step out the back of the motel and walk on the beach. I was warm, amazed, and happy...until in the middle of our trip, when I woke up on the morning of the fourth night of Chanukah.

Knowing Chanukah was coming, my parents had remembered to bring along a menorah and some gelt—no problem there. We were staying in a very modest motel with lots of red and green decorations and pictures of Jesus adorning the lobby. There in front of the Christmas tree, my oldest sister, Marilyn, lit the menorah on the first night of Chanukah. Sherry, who was the next-oldest, got to light it the second night, and Joanne, being next in line, took her turn on the third night. The other motel guests seemed both curious and respectful of our evening rituals. It was an interesting, mellow scene.

The morning of the fourth night was when the fireworks started. It was then that I realized I was the fourth child, the fourth night was coming, and, unlike my sisters, I didn't know the candle blessings. I went berserk, as only a six-year-old can. I wanted my turn, and no amount of "Say-it-in-English" or "Repeat-after-me" appeasement would work. If it was good enough for my sisters, it was good enough for me, and I was perfectly prepared to keep crying until I got my way or suffered a brain hemorrhage—whichever came first.

Catching wind of my jealousy and angst, my father came to the rescue. He took me by the hand and led me to the beach. What followed was one of the simplest but most memorable events of my childhood. Two guys in baggy shorts, one six, one thirty-four, walked hand in hand up and down the beach, over and over and over again. While we walked along the hot sand and cooled our toes in the foamy surf, my dad kept saying the Chanukah candle blessings to me and having me say them back to him. It went on for at least four or five hours. Later that night, I took my turn at the menorah and felt proud. Thanks to my dad, I belonged.

Two thousand years ago, Jews had a choice to leave Judaism for the gymnasium: we have the same choice today. Back then, the battle for Jewish survival was fought by soldiers with swords; today by every Jewish parent through long walks and patient teaching. Blessings have to be repeated, and Judaism has to be lived to be learned: who will do this for children if not their parents?

Born about twenty-one centuries too late, I suppose my father wasn't exactly a Maccabee...but in December 1966, with my hand in his, he managed to quietly re-create their miracle and help fight their war. I hope the rest of us with children do too.

Quiet Miracles

From the moving silence of trees, whether in
storm or calm, in leaf and naked, night or day,
we draw conclusions of our own, sustaining and
unnoticed as our breath.

HOWARD NEMEROV

For centuries, Jews have gathered on Tu B'Shevat—the fifteenth day of the Hebrew month Shevat—to celebrate the first blossoms of spring, dedicate their orchards to God, feast on fifteen different fruits in a special Tu B'Shevat seder, and, above all, to recognize the value of trees. Most people dismiss Tu B'Shevat as a quaint reminder of our people's agrarian past. Sure, we know, trees matter to our ecosystem and, our fresh-squeezed orange juice, but they're not really important to us in a personal way. To most, a holiday dedicated to trunks and branches seems a little absurd.

Never mind that in the Torah, it was a tree that held knowledge. It was an olive branch brought back to Noah's ark by a dove that marked the earth's renewal. Today an olive branch still represents peace across the world. We use palm fronds, an *etrog*, and branches of willow and myrtle to celebrate Sukkot. Many traditional Jews plant a tree when their child is born and later, when the child marries, use its branches for the chuppah poles. The Torah itself, the most sacred possession of the Jewish people, is called an *Etz Chayim*—a Tree of Life.

The oldest living things on earth, the longest-surviving remnants of God's original Creation, born before the pharaohs ruled Egypt, are bristlecone pine trees in northern California. Although most of them measure less than thirty feet tall, they are at least 4,600 years old and still alive. The tallest living thing on earth is a California sequoia standing 290 feet, measuring 80 feet in girth, weighing over 6,000 tons, and estimated to be 2,500 years old.

The average tree produces 240 pounds of oxygen a year and absorbs the pollution caused by burning a ton of coal. Trees give shade to other plants and animals—including human beings. They hold the earth's rivers in their banks and topsoil in its place. Trees produce almost all of our fruit and nuts, cool the globe, and sustain life as we know it on our planet. Trees are miracles.

There are many important trees in my life. There was the sapling my dad and I dug up in the Minnesota woods and planted in the front yard when I was nine. That little tree, now a towering elm, is the first thing I see when I pull into the driveway during my visits home. To me, it represents the steady progress of time, rooting me to my childhood home, my past, my father. There was the tree I used to climb to smooch in when I was twelve and the apple trees we planted in the backyard after each of my grandparents died.

But the most important tree of all stands in front of a tiny apartment in Katamon—a Jerusalem slum full of children, cats, and broken windows—where Gali lives. I volunteered to become Gali's big brother one month after his father was killed in Lebanon. He was nine, his brother eleven, his sister seven, and his mother, a widow at thirty-three. I was a lonely twenty-two-year-old student far from home. We still write to each other.

Dear Gali,

I'm trying to write about how much our tree and being brothers mean to us. But I doubt people will ever know how scared we both were that afternoon we met. I knew about ten words in Hebrew, and you, an angry, brokenhearted nine-year-old, knew even less English. You taught me hundreds of words as we built our tree house together in front of your apartment.

Remember how we snuck through the neighborhood stealing scraps of wood? Remember the little platform and the splintered, crooked steps nailed into the trunk? Feet dangling, hands laced behind our heads, leaning back in the warm Jerusalem sun like two old men, we'd sit for hours atop the branches. "What a view we have," you used to brag, "what a view."

We talked a lot about your dad in that tree, about how you sometimes saw him in your dreams promising he'd come back. I think the time you took me to see his grave and to say Kaddish, just the two of us, is the day we really became brothers.

I remember the trips to the beach, the soccer games in the park, kick-the-can and hide-and-seek, Ima's stuffed grape leaves, the hot tea with sugar and mint on cold winter nights, the laughs, the tears. Understanding your emptiness without having to say it; loving you without having to prove it.

The Torah is full of miraculous plagues and liberation, war, blood, and salvation—pure power unleashed. The world can be a fast, harsh place...making us fast and harsh too. But the Jewish calendar calls us to recognize the harvest of slower, humbler miracles...the kind of miracles that are hard to find behind brick and glass, gates and security alarms, the kind of miracles that come instead from climbing upward and noticing, from trunks and swaying branches calming us down by lifting us toward what God really intended us to be—quiet and together.

Oh, to be leaning back in the warm Jerusalem sun again, Gali, fingers laced behind our heads, feet dangling, like two old men—real friends, brothers. What a view we had. What a view.

CHAPTER 5

Judaism

There is no room for God in someone who is filled with himself.

BA'AL SHEM TOV

A FRIEND TOLD ME about a scene he witnessed recently at a delicatessen. A woman who apparently was not Jewish was standing in line at the bakery counter. When they called her number, she pointed to the prune and poppy-seed hamantashen and asked for a dozen.

"No, you want these," advised the elderly Jewish woman who was serving her, pointing to the apricot hamantashen instead.

"No, I want those," the woman reiterated, pointing again to the prune and poppy-seed variety.

"Honey, these you will like," the Jewish woman replied, pointing again to the apricot flavor. "Those," she said, looking at the prune and poppy-seed tray, "need an acquired taste."

An acquired taste—enjoyment or understanding resulting from regular exposure—is something Jews have appreciated from the beginning. Remember what happened at Mount Sinai? A cloud descends from the mountaintop, a strange brew of mist and ash. Moses appears from out of the cloud, takes a long, sweeping look before he speaks, and then, in one mighty blast, laws tumble forth from his stony face—an avalanche of statutes and ordinances, thou-shalts and shalt-nots.

When Moses finished, as if in some great, unrehearsed symphony, the six-hundred-thousand Jews listening to him shouted, *"Na-a-seh v-nish-ma"*: We will do and we will listen. From the start, Jews affirmed that in order to really understand Judaism, they had to practice it. I often tell my students who are converting to Judaism that becoming a Jew is like learning to swim—a textbook only takes you so far. A student behind a desk can read every book ever written on swimming, see every instructional video, hear the best motivational speakers, and then, no matter how lengthy or extensive their training, enter the deep end of a pool and quickly drown.

Everyone understands the difference between learning and doing in swimming, and in many other things too. How many times have your kids stared at something on their plate and heard you say, "Try it—it's good"? How many of us really enjoyed our first beer? We readily accept that our first trip to the symphony might not captivate or inspire us, but if we work at it, each concert gets better. We have to study, read up, and ask questions. Any skill that enhances our life and brings us pleasure—painting, playing the piano, even a decent game of tennis—takes time, effort, and practice. Most Jews understand this fact of life...except when it comes to Judaism.

Many among us want simple answers to tough personal and societal questions. People want "spirituality" without taking the time to acquire the religious knowledge and skill that real spirituality demands; they want the keys to inner doors of wisdom without first unlocking the outer doors of study and practice. I hear it almost daily; every rabbi does. "Rabbi, I'm not very religious, and I don't know or do very much, but I *feel* Jewish, and that's the important thing."

To this statement I usually reply, "I'm not very knowledgeable and haven't practiced at all, but I *feel* like a doctor. Why not let me try bypass surgery on you?" The two statements, it seems to me, are equally absurd. It's not that feelings are unimportant. Pride in our heritage as Jews is crucial. But if it's pride without any real understanding or commitment, then it's false pride. *Feeling* Jewish is not enough.

New Age religion, minimalist Judaism, easy answers, and reactionary social policies are meager responses, mere avoidances of the real effort required to find meaning. Judaism isn't easy. Seeking meaning involves living, praying, making Shabbat, giving tzedakah, mourning, celebrating, and even eating as a Jew.

Our ancestors understood that action preceded insight, and effort necessarily came before reward. It's an equation that seemed clear to them and seems equally clear to many of us in every aspect of life except our spirituality. Why do we deny that Jews who want to find meaning in their tradition have to put forth at least as much regular effort as Jews who want to improve their golf games? The woman behind the deli counter was right: Judaism *is* an acquired taste. We have to try it over and over again to discover just how sweet it is.

A Happy New Age Tune

Am I my brother's keeper?

CAIN

In honor of our tenth anniversary and in the interest of being a good sport, I agreed to two days of "treatments" and "renewal" at a well-known, understated spa in the California desert. It's a hippie-gone-New-Age kind of place with mindless flute music and candles at every turn. Don't get me wrong. I like slipping into a mineral hot spring and having warm oil rubbed into my scalp by a woman in Birkenstocks as much as the next guy, but this place was weird. Consider the "treatments":

There was the Native American, which involved brushing your body with eucalyptus branches, rubbing "healing" herbs blended with corn oil into your muscles, and wrapping you in a warm herbal sheet while chanting Native American blessings. The Egyptian Clay treatment "...cleanses your body of physical, emotional, and spiritual toxicity." The Reflexology promised to "...break up crystallization and dissolve blocked energy." And let's not forget the renowned Wassertanzen, during which, according to the spa's brochure, "feelings of complete trust and relaxation surface as your therapist leads you underwater using massage, baby rocking, dolphin and dance movements.... Deep states unfold within you as you surrender to yourself."

Stranger only than the "treatments" were some of the guests at this oasis of heightened consciousness. Other than having the same blissed-out look on their faces, they were a pretty diverse bunch. Among them: a TV actor and his wife who spent most of their time rubbing each other's feet; a famous folksinger who drove a Porsche and said "far out" a lot; a Hollywood exec and his quite-young, quite-blonde "friend"; two old-women hippies just back from hiking in China; a writer from New York; and a couple from Santa Fe who told me they considered Wassertanzen "very important work," and that since Venus and the moon were in the perfect positions, their massage experience was going to be "prime."

The folks at this spa represent just a small segment of the people who subscribe to New Age rites of passage. There are tens of thousands more, and, truth be told, Jews are a huge part of the movement. In fact, it's estimated that one-third or more of the Americans who journey to India to study with a spiritual master are Jews.

I've never gone to India, and while I only spent two days among the devotees of this New Age spa, what I discovered there bothered me. Sure, I joined in the quiet, blissful fun with a few treatments of my own. I, too, showed up for dinner in my bathrobe looking dazed and at peace. I relaxed. I enjoyed myself. But then it was over. Before I knew it, I was back to my life as a rabbi.

Barbara needed checking up on—she was fighting cancer and complications that landed her in intensive care for almost two months. This mother of three was barely hanging on. Wendy was finally pregnant after years of infertility treatments—she just wanted me to hear the good news. Marty, a mere boy of eighteen, was going in for his marrow transplant—his chances were about thirty-eight percent—his mother wanted to talk. There was Torah to teach and the marrying and burying to do.

It turns out that there's a difference between Betsy and me, who returned to reality, and many of the spa's other guests. Many weren't just visiting the Dream State of Inner Peace; they were full-time citizens, going from spa to spa, seminar to guru, mud bath to watsu pool, cold cucumber wrap to crystals, and psychic to astrologer. They have plenty of money, time, and most of all, an unceasing interest in their own well-being to the exclusion of just about everything else. As far as I can tell, for these people and many who emulate them, the New Age pretty much boils down to "Me, me, me—far out!"

What's worse than the truly lost people who wind up there are the serious, successful people who have been sucked into New Age through its mirage of quick wisdom or hidden insight immediately revealed through the right seminar or sage. While not exactly superstitious, these seekers look for, and think they've found, a brand of speedy magic to make their lives more meaningful.

How Jewish is this New Age? Not very. Just remember what the Talmud has to say about the Jews who are singing and dancing, celebrating their miraculous escape from Pharaoh across the Sea of Reeds. According to the Talmud, even the angels in heaven wanted to break forth into song upon seeing the Jews rescued and the Egyptians crushed beneath the ocean waves. But God scolds the angels, saying, "The work of my hands is drowning in the sea, and you want to sing!" It's the Talmud's little reminder that Jews should never be so wrapped up in their own pleasure that they ignore the pain of others. That's why we remove ten drops of wine from our cups during our Passover seders—to remind us of the suffering each plague brought to the Egyptians—rejoicing while others suffer is not Jewish.

I met many people at the spa who whistle a happy New Age tune while they ignore the rest of God's creatures all around them; people who are so busy cultivating their own inner peace that they never confront the world outside. To be a Jew is to know the world needs us, all of us. Sure, everyone likes a nice vacation and a good massage, but I've met too many people who never snap out of it.

I suppose New Agers consider their search for a constant state of bliss an admirable one. I, for one, was happy to spend a few days relaxing but even happier to return to the real world with all its opportunities to do good; it's where we belong. Because Wassertanzen may be many things, but it is not "very important work."

The Most Important Lesson

Whatever is in your power to do, do with
all your might.

ECCLESIASTES

My father, Leonard, was not a Torah scholar. He was a blue-collar sort of guy who, throughout my childhood, went to work in steel-toed boots and a uniform that said "Len" on it. He barely finished high school. But here's how smart he was.

When I was five years old and wanted a toy, my dad had me shine his dress shoes for a dime a pair. At ten years old, I went to work with him every Saturday morning, cleaning the toilets and floors at the scrap yard he owned with my uncle Mort; no mop or machines, just a pail and a scrub brush. My knees and hands hurt at the end of the day.

Each summer, I wire-brushed the rust off the dumpsters used to hold metal at the scrap yard. Afterward I painted them black; no paint guns or sprayers, just a roller and a pan. One of those summers, my brother and I spent the evenings crawling in the attic of our Minnesota home, pouring bags of insulation into the rafters. It was over 100° up there, and we sneezed out black dust at the end of each shift. Sometimes I slopped tar on the roofs of my father's warehouses in the hot August sun. Once I helped roof our house. Sometimes I mixed cement by hand in a wheelbarrow to patch the sidewalk. Sure, we could have rented a cement mixer. But my father preferred that I use the "arm-strong" method, as he liked to put it. Then there was that infamous summer when after I had been arrested for shoplifting, my father decided I would be rehabilitated by forgoing camp in order to spend the time spreading huge piles of dirt on our lawn with a shovel and a rake.

The Extraordinary Nature of Ordinary Things

My dad was the kind of guy who'd come outside when I was playing with my friends in the street and make me go back into the yard to reweed around the shrubs because I hadn't done it right the first time. He was also the kind of guy who'd do the same thing again because I hadn't done it right the second time either. Believe me, by the third time, you couldn't find a weed around those shrubs with a microscope and tweezers.

Dad's solution to every problem, great or small, was always annoyingly simple and unshakable—work harder. Although he would not have put it this way, for my father, work was redemptive and holy. For my father, work was God; I, Steven, son of Leonard, was raised in the Temple of Sweat.

In a way, it's similar to the ancient rabbis' use of the book of Leviticus in the Torah. The first lessons in a Jewish school were not the magical, wonderful, exciting stories of Creation, Adam and Eve, Noah, Abraham and Sarah, Moses, plagues and parting seas, but rather, this grisly, boring book about the sacrifices offered up by our ancestors to God on the altar of the ancient Temple in Jerusalem. In the rabbis' opinion, the archaic, ancient, seemingly irrelevant book of Leviticus had the most important and relevant lesson of all to teach our children. Leviticus is a reminder to do the dirty work, to make real sacrifices, then, and only then, as our tradition teaches, reap the rewards.

It wasn't easy being my father's son, pulling weeds while other kids played in the street. But now I realize that anything I have or will become is a result of the lessons he taught me about hard work. And I realize, too, that we really only care about the things we are willing to sacrifice for. It's the same lesson the ancient rabbis wanted all Jewish children to learn.

Like I said, my father was no Torah scholar, but boy was he smart.

The Tefillin in the Basement

Anyone who understands his foolishness is already a little wiser.

YIDDISH PROVERB

M y older cousin, Earl, was into Judaism in a big way when I was a kid. I mean, he was cool and everything—played guitar, had long hair, a beard, earth shoes, and his own room in the attic—but the guy loved to pray. This made him something of an exception in the Leder clan.

Since then, Earl's gone on to write a couple of great books about Judaism and morality. He teaches Torah all over Minneapolis and St. Paul and is generally renowned for his brilliance and his *menschlichkeit*. I respect him for all of that, but more so, for something he did when his thirteen-year-old little cousin became a bar mitzvah...something I am sure he has forgotten by now.

Digging through the packages and envelopes of my post-bar-mitzvah-party loot twenty-five years ago, I unearthed a small box with a card on top from Earl. "I know that you probably won't use these," it said, "but every Jew should have them just in case."

I opened the box to discover two smaller boxes, shiny and black, with stiff leather straps. I'd seen tefillin in pictures and on the praying Chasid curios for sale in the temple gift shop. But these were mine, and one thing Earl had said in his card was for sure—I wouldn't use them.

For more than a decade, the tefillin I never used stayed inside the velvet bag that held the tallis I never wore, on the shelf in the basement bedroom of my parents' home where I no longer lived. I couldn't bring myself to throw these

The Extraordinary Nature of Ordinary Things

artifacts of an irrelevant Judaism from an unenlightened era away, but I had no use for them either. Until my liturgy professor in rabbinical school gave us an assignment—three weeks of praying at an Orthodox shul.

"Mom, send those tefillin in the basement, will ya?"

I've been a proud Reform Jew my entire life. I'm an unapologetic "spirit of the law trumps the letter of the law" sort of guy. I drive to synagogue on Shabbat, believe in egalitarian Judaism, full rights for homosexuals, and that Jewish law is important but not the only consideration in making religious decisions. Had you asked what my reaction to wearing tefillin would have been before I tried them, I would have answered you with the words of the Reform movement's Torah commentary on the verses about tefillin, which states: "Reform Jews stress internal commitment over adherence to external forms. . . . The biblical prescription to 'place a sign upon your hand and a reminder upon your forehead' was meant in a figurative way only." Yep, that was me, Mr. Rational. Until I tried it.

Figurative or not, there's something powerful about literally placing a tiny box filled with promises of redemption from the Torah onto your upper arm facing your heart. Wrapping the thin black strap seven times around your arm and finishing it off in the shape of a *shin*—the first letter of God's name—laced between your fingers is meditative and connecting; it connects you to the other men by your side, the Torah, the past, God. A shining black square suspended just below your hairline with leather straps cascading over your shoulders really does remind you of who and what you are.

Fifteen years after those experimental days in rabbinical school, not always, not even often, but sometimes, I wrap myself in my tallis and my tefillin, sway to a rhythm unheard, and lose myself in a world of ancient words. I guess I've learned what Cousin Earl knew all along: not always, but sometimes, what's rational isn't what's meaningful, and what once we dismissed, we may later embrace. Certain things are worth keeping, as Earl himself might put it, "just in case."

Why Jews Should Not Celebrate Christmas

American banker Otto Kahn was Jewish by birth but had converted to Christianity. He was once walking with a hunchbacked friend when they passed a synagogue.

"You know I used to be a Jew," Kahn said.

"And I used to be a hunchback," his companion replied.

M y son discovered Christmas when he was three-and-a-half years old. He wanted to know what those trees and lights were all about; who that jolly, bearded man in the red suit putting children on his lap at the mall was. "I want to see him, Daddy," he pleaded as only a three-and-a-half-year-old can.

"Once, just once, I want to have a tree in our house," my friend's seven-year-old daughter informed her.

"Rabbi," a congregant recently said to me, "my son just started public school, and he's very upset that he can't have Christmas. What should I tell him?"

I suppose almost everything that needs to be said about Jews and Christmas has already been articulated by many people in many places. Yet when parents are first confronted with the problem in their own families, it's still just that: a first. Often we simply don't know enough honest, thoughtful answers to help our children cope with Christmas.

Furthermore, the problem of Jews and Christmas runs far deeper than our children. Many adult Jews celebrate Christmas either because they are part of an interfaith relationship or simply because they were raised in a Jewish home where Christmas was celebrated, and they like it just fine.

Christmas in America, with all of its spirit and merry-making, its generosity and goodwill, makes Jewish children, and many adults, feel like outsiders. They want in; they want to be like everyone else. Even some who resist the urge to celebrate still have a nagging desire to join in the holiday spirit.

The problem is that when Jews celebrate Christmas, we work against some of our most important Jewish ideals, not the least of which is ensuring the Jewish identity of our children. Celebrating Christmas confuses children. I know—years later, I see a lot of them in my office for counseling. They can't understand why their parents, who raised them embracing Jewish and Christian holidays, are suddenly so surprised when they choose a non-Jewish spouse.

If you are part of an interfaith couple with children and are celebrating Christmas and Chanukah in an attempt to raise them in both religious traditions, don't kid yourself. You might end up with children who feel neither Jewish nor Christian. Don't heap your own ambiguities upon your children. Make a consistent and clear choice about their religious upbringing. Children deserve and need their parents to be consistent and clear.

One of the often overlooked but most disturbing things about Jews celebrating Christmas is that it is insulting to Christians. Christmas is a religious holiday many of them take seriously. It is a day of piety, prayer, and hope. Jews have no right to appropriate and trivialize Christmas by proclaiming it "just a day to celebrate with family, decorate the tree, and exchange gifts." If Christians want to dismiss the religious significance of Christmas, that's one thing; for Jews to do it is quite another.

Of course, most Jews who celebrate Christmas do so for the simple reason that they want to be like everyone else in America. Guess what? Celebrating Christmas won't make you like your Christian neighbors any more than visiting a poultry farm makes you a chicken.

When Jews no longer appreciate the opportunity to be different, when our primary concern is to "fit in," we ultimately deny much of what has kept our people alive for thousands of years. Our winter holiday, Chanukah, was and is about holding on to Judaism against the whims of popular culture. Chanukah is about the miracle of Jewish survival achieved by resisting the need to be like everyone else. It's a miracle worth celebrating...and worth protecting too.

Just a Moment

I walked into my mother's room, and she was
cleaning out everything, and she was crying.
I tried to hold her. Some other times, before
that, when I saw her crying, I went in and started
crying with her. It's made us closer than we
were before.

LAURIE MARSHALL, AGE 12

I am a very young rabbi. People even joke about it. "The only rabbi in history who hasn't had his bar mitzvah yet," they say. Okay, so I'm a kid, ordained at the age of twenty-six, the youngest in my class. But in my short time as a rabbi, I have seen and buried more than my share of bodies, hundreds of them. I will never be young again.

Some drifted into a dark and peaceful sleep at the end of a life well lived. Others journeyed through the pain, the degradation, the unrelenting attack of cancer. One was twenty-six, a car accident. Another twenty-two, AIDS. Some left no children or lover to mourn them. Some left family and friends behind in shock, in anger, in a loneliness more profound and deep than words can say. We gather around the dinner table, and loved ones, once present, are gone. Each holiday, each celebration, is mingled with a yearning and a sadness beyond belief.

Yet somehow we manage to go on. Each morning, we put on our masks of normalcy, our clothes of contentment, and we step out into the world of those who do not mourn. We are dizzy from the pain of loneliness, but somehow we have learned to stand up in it. And then, in the strangest places and the oddest moments, it all comes rushing back. The deathwatch at the hospital. The faceless doctors. The masks, the gowns, the gloves. The phone calls, the confusion, the exhaustion, the funeral, the coffin, the clods of earth, the depression, and the tears.

So we come to synagogue; we rise with the others who mourn; we face the hurt and the sorrow all over again. We remember our loved ones, and we recite words of Kaddish—every day for the first eleven months. Five times a year after that, we light a memorial candle, we pray and remember. And what, in the face of such tender memory and prayer, what in the face of such terrible loneliness and despair, is a rabbi to say? What message will make a difference? What words will crown such a moment with meaning?

The answer, at least in part it seems to me, can be found not in what the rabbi or our tradition have to say but in what they do not say, in the answers we do not pretend to have. Never trust a religion or a person with all the answers. Trust instead in the religion and people who admit there are things we can never know, simply because we are human. Know what not to say. "Please," wrote a woman who lost her daughter in a car accident, "don't ask me if I'm over it yet. I'll never be over it."

Please: Don't tell me she's in a better place. She isn't here.

Please: Don't say, at least she isn't suffering. I haven't come to terms with why she had to suffer at all.

Please: Don't tell me how I feel unless you have lost a child.

Please: Don't tell me to get on with my life. I'm still here, you'll notice.

Please: Don't ask me if I feel better. Bereavement isn't a condition that clears up.

Please: Don't tell me God never makes a mistake. You mean God did this on purpose?

Please: Don't tell me at least you had her for twenty-eight years. What year would you choose for your daughter to die?

Please: Don't tell me God never gives you more than you can bear. Who decides how much another person can bear?
Please: Just say you are sorry.
Please: Just say you remember her if you do.
Please: Just let me talk if I want to.
Please: Let me cry when I must.

Kaddish and memory are not about easy answers to tough questions. Judaism is not about why people must die. It's not about taking away the pain and the ache. It's not about rationalizing away the loss of loved ones who enriched our lives beyond measure. Faith can't do that. New Age religion can't do that. The rabbi can't do that. Nothing can do that. Judaism knows better, and so do people who mourn. To pretend that such pain can be explained away, that answers to such questions exist, that we will "get over it" isn't fair; it isn't fair to our grief and our anguish. It isn't fair to our loved ones.

No, Judaism is not about such things. It's about taking time for our sorrow. It's about our memories. It's about our human need to talk and to cry. It's about taking off our masks of normalcy. When we rise to say Kaddish, we do not rise to say we are over it; we do not say we understand. Death is a mystery beyond our grasp, and there are no easy answers. There is only what each of us really needs. A moment to say our loved ones meant something to us we can never put into words. A moment to say that although we have gone on with our lives, we will remember them always; that they counted, that their life mattered. No easy answers. Just a moment to remember, to talk, to cry. Just a moment, please.

CHAPTER 6

Marriage

Love consists in this, that two solitudes protect and touch and greet each other.

RAINER MARIA RILKE

THE MIDRASH SAYS THAT poverty is the worst of all afflictions. But I think it's something else—loneliness. Human beings are lonely creatures, craving love. I see it in the eyes of elderly men who lose their wives of half a century or more. I see it in the longing and desperation of women in their forties who can not seem to find the right man. We all want to reach out to someone who will reach out to us. We all want love.

It's not that marriage is a guarantee against loneliness. There are plenty of married people who are lonely; who, because of the mortgage, the children, or the lack of will, suffer but tough it out. It's just that marriage is a calculated and magical approach to fighting loneliness that seems to work better than any other.

I remember when my parents told their five children they were getting divorced. We were gathered around the dinner table, red sauce on white spaghetti noodles covering my plate. How like my mother to feed us, to do her duty, before delivering bad news.

"I think we have to talk," my father said. Then, for the first time in my life, I saw him cry. My mother wanted freedom; he wanted to stay. No, neither of them had cheated on the other. Dad would get an apartment nearby. Mom would make him a soup for us to bring when we visited. I was fourteen, and in my adolescent simplicity, I asked them only one question: "Do you love each other?"

I don't think they answered. At least, I don't remember their answer. I do remember the look on their faces. It was a look that said: "You are only fourteen. You have much to learn. Marriage is not as simple as love."

I told my dad to get a big enough apartment for me, too, because I was going with him. Two of my older sisters tore into my mother and told her if she was so unhappy, she could move out of the house, and we'd bring her a nice soup. The Leder children were not going to take this lying down. We united, we protested, we sulked, and we succeeded. Somehow, after seeing our reactions, my parents realized that they had built more together than they'd thought and that the downside of loneliness was steep. They decided to fight for their marriage. So far, it has lasted forty-eight years.

At fourteen, because it was almost snatched away, I learned that marriage was not the perfect or the only answer to the human condition, but it was the best answer. Since then, I've come to appreciate even more how men and women need each other and how much children need them both. I've come to appreciate the role God and destiny play in the miracle of human love and how lucky we are to find what other creatures on earth lack.

When I stand under the chuppah with couples, I always remind them that their wedding is not their marriage, that a marriage doesn't happen on a particular day or place. A marriage is built through months and years of laughter, toil, illness, adventure, sex, lack of sex, rest, no rest, understanding, confusion, and forgiveness. I remind grooms that the Talmud says, "If your wife is shorter than you, bend down, and listen to her"; husband and wife must try to understand each other with all their might. I remind them that the Hebrew word for marriage is *kiddushin*, from the Hebrew *kadosh*, meaning holy or separate. If they treat each other as *kadosh*—sacred, fragile vessels, easily shattered—they'll be able to hang on, snuggled beneath the blanket of years, come what may.

Then, when all the words have been spoken, they break a glass to remember there will also be sadness. They kiss. They feast. They dance, and they love. Later, if they are lucky and devoted, they will find another kind of love, built together through the years; a richer, deeper love...a love that is a marriage.

Daddy and Mommy, Sittin' in a Tree...

Chains do not hold a marriage together.
It is threads, hundreds of tiny threads, which
sew people together through the years.

SIMONE SIGNORET

"Hey, Dad, listen to this!" my son, Aaron, says with a gleam in his eye. "Daddy and Mommy sittin' in a tree, k-i-s-s-i-n-g. First comes love, then comes marriage, then comes Daddy with the baby carriage." Aaron learned the rhyme from a friend at school who convinced him it was an original creation. He was so proud of his little ditty that I didn't have the heart to tell him it's known to practically everyone in the English-speaking world. I also didn't tell him that according to the Torah, the whole thing is wrong anyway.

When Abraham's wife, Sarah, dies, the Torah describes his despair. What must it have been like for him after fifty or sixty years of marriage to wake up in a bed half empty, yearning for the warmth and the touch, for the sparkling eyes and the comfort, of his life's partner? What was it like to bury the woman who believed in him and held him in her arms? Abraham's first love, his only love—gone.

So what does Abraham do after losing his precious life's partner? According to the Torah, after burying Sarah and mourning her loss, Abraham immediately instructs his servant to find a wife for his son Isaac. After losing Sarah, Abraham realizes just how much she meant to him and how important it is for his son to share his life with a woman of equal character.

So off goes Abraham's servant to find a wife for Isaac. Stopping at a well in the desert, the servant sees Rebecca. Her skin is dark olive; she is young, graceful, and soft. Rebecca offers him water and then waters his camels as well. It was not her beauty but her kindness toward the servant and his animals that made Rebecca a suitable wife for Isaac.

After the servant negotiates with her family, Rebecca agrees to travel with him to meet Isaac and become his wife. At journey's end, she sees Isaac walking alone in a distant field. He is grieving and suffering from his mother's death, walking in a loneliness aching and dark. Then, as the Torah simply puts it: "He took Rebecca as his wife. Isaac loved her, and he was comforted after his mother's death."

It all sounds sweet and romantic. But actually, if you stop to think about it, the Torah seems to have things a little backward. Shouldn't it have said that Isaac loved Rebecca and then took her as his wife? Isn't "first comes love, then comes marriage..." the way we tend to think about these things, even in first grade? Why is the Torah different?

Anyone who's been married for a decade or two, or six, knows the answer. If you had asked me at the time of my own wedding whether or not I loved my wife, Betsy, I would have said "yes" only because I didn't know then what I know now. It takes a certain kind of affection to start a marriage—but it takes a deeper, more seasoned love to make it last. Marriage isn't something that happens to us on a particular day or in a particular place. Weddings don't make people married. Weddings are beginnings; marriages are journeys. It takes years, even decades, to truly love someone.

When we were first married, I never knew that Betsy would be such a remarkable mother and that I would admire her so much for it. I never knew that when our marriage would begin to crack under the strain of the rabbinate, it would be Betsy who would have the courage to force us to get help. No one could have told me about the simple pleasure of sleeping side by side with her for fourteen years, fit together like two spoons beneath the warm covers.

One morning, while I was walking out the door on my way to the cemetery to bury a child, Betsy looked at me and said: "If anyone can help this family, you can." When I married her, I could never have imagined how much her believing in me would make a difference in my life.

It's not just Betsy and me; it's any couple that has built a life together despite the struggles and disappointments they sometimes bring to each other. Any couple that has overcome the lack of time, money, and sleep, the pettiness, the stubbornness, and the illnesses, realizes that love grows out of the balance between these realities and the secret laughter, the gentle touch, a first home, a midnight moment watching children sleep silently in their beds, marveling at every breath.

To those of us who have hung in there with each other over the years, it's pretty clear that the old nursery rhyme had it wrong, and the Torah had it right all along. When he's old enough to understand, I want my little boy, Aaron, to know the truth about that rhyme; about Isaac and Rebecca, his mom and dad, and the rest of us too. A wedding is a beginning, marriage is a journey, and love takes time.

Abe, Molly, Passover, and Life

*I know I have felt oppressed as a Jew. Like the
time the heater went out on my pool.*

COMEDIAN ADAM SANDLER

M any people think eating matzah instead of *chametz*
(leaven) is the hardest part of Passover. I think the hardest part isn't what we're supposed to eat or not eat but how
we're supposed to feel. The haggadah commands that each
of us is supposed to consider ourselves as having been
personally redeemed from slavery. But if we are really
supposed to feel redeemed, then we must first feel imprisoned
and oppressed. And that's the problem.

Sure, there's plenty of oppression in the world. There are
plenty of others to think about on Passover. But that's not all
the haggadah says. The haggadah doesn't only instruct us to
think about others as oppressed—it says we must think of *ourselves* as oppressed. But when we compare our own problems
to those of the world's truly downtrodden, for most of us, seeing
ourselves as oppressed may be a pretty difficult stretch.

But, a few months ago, I came face-to-face with a reason
Passover matters to each of us every year. It was a beautiful
day, really—one of those perfect California days—sun, clear
sky, fresh, cool air. I was on my way to visit Abe. Actually,
it was more than a visit. Abe's son called me a few days
earlier to tell me that Molly had died. Abe and Molly had been
married for sixty-four years, and she had taken care of him
after his stroke. A few months ago, Molly suffered a stroke
too. Since then, she and Abe had shared the same room in
the nursing home. They had lain side by side, unable to speak
except an occasional simple word.

Abe and Molly spent day after day searching each other's dulled eyes for sparks of a life once brilliant and alive. And now Molly was gone—buried a day before in Northern California while Abe remained behind, hunched in his wheelchair, trapped in a pale-yellow room with a shiny floor, dirty curtains, a picture, a bedpan, and a towel tucked under his chin.

I found Abe with his two children and two others who had come to help him say goodbye to Molly. I, too, had come to help him say goodbye, to say Kaddish, to give his sweet Molly's life meaning and voice in our people's ancient way. But Abe was beyond comfort. Each time I mentioned Molly's name, he arched back in his wheelchair and stretched his mouth wide—he wanted to speak, to cry out, to scream—but the stroke had robbed him of everything except his grimace and his gape. Still, we said Kaddish. We talked of Molly and her love for life. We assured Abe and each other that she was better off now. But Abe just moaned.

It was a long, quiet drive back to the temple. I turned off the radio because I wanted to think, to be sad, to absorb whatever truth about life and death I'd discovered in Abe's room. My visit with him answered my Passover dilemma, the question posed by the wicked son in the haggadah who asks, "What does this holiday have to do with you?" the question of every one of us who is not hungry, homeless, sick, or alone—who wonders what, if anything, enslaves us?

The answer was in that dreary room and in Abe's face. We may not be hungry, homeless, or imprisoned, but we are prisoners. We are all prisoners of time. That's why it's hard to visit a nursing home. That's why Abe aches. Life runs out. Being oppressed by time is a simple truth we try not to think about. But it's true nonetheless—just ask Abe.

In his book *Lessons for Living,* Sidney Greenberg cites a study by psychologist William Marston who asked three thousand people this brief question: "What do you have to live for?" He found that ninety-four percent of his respondents were simply enduring the present while they waited for the future. They were waiting for: "something to happen—waiting for the right man or the right woman; waiting for children to grow up; waiting to pay off the mortgage; waiting for a vacation; waiting for retirement; waiting to get involved in the community; waiting to learn some new skill or hobby." Ninety-four percent of us are waiting while each new day passes us by; one-hundred percent of us are running out of time.

Every year, we sit around the seder table heaped with laughter, song, and good food—we ponder the wicked son's question and wonder what it all has to do with us. Perhaps we ought to ponder Abe and Molly too, who come to teach us that we have no time to waste. We simply have each brief day to give our lives meaning against the shackles of time, each brief day to share our hearts, our warmth, and our love.

CHAPTER 7

Unfinished Business

Every human being may become righteous.

MOSES MAIMONIDES

EVERY YEAR BEFORE YOM KIPPUR, a rabbi gathered his family and friends along with every member of his Board of Trustees, put them in a room, and announced:

"If I've done or said anything at all this past year to offend you or hurt your feelings, I just want to say that you're too sensitive!"

Of course it's a joke, but the fact that most of us will do almost anything to avoid facing up to our shortcomings is no laughing matter. Self-scrutiny is hard to take. It's tough to come to temple on Yom Kippur and admit that we have been wrong. We can be cruel. We can be sarcastic. We can be dishonest. We are hurtful and stubborn. Worst of all, these sins are usually as true of us each new year as they were the last. With our *Avinu Malkeinus* and our *Al Cheits*, we promise to vanquish our foolishness, our petty gossip, our hurtful ways with the ones we love. Each Yom Kippur there is so much unfinished business in our lives, and although we swear that by the next Yom Kippur things will be different, we're wrong.

And what unfinished business we have: the weight we haven't lost, the working out we haven't begun, the times we were going to go to temple, the credit card bills we haven't paid off, the garage that isn't straightened up, the dentist appointment we haven't made yet, the books stacked on our nightstand waiting to be read. We've *all* got those pieces of unfinished business that nag us and mock our good intentions, our empty words, and our broken promises.

The unfinished business in our families and our friendships haunts most of us just below the surface of our lives. And each Yom Kippur, we are supposed to rise above our

The Extraordinary Nature of Ordinary Things

indifference and our denial. It's a day to come clean, to face our past, and to vow to remake our future. If we are really interested in more than empty prayer on the High Holy Days, if we are really interested in *teshuvah*, in repentance and redemption, in salvation, then we must do more than merely pray about making things right with others—we must actually try to do it. Our tradition teaches us that Jews ought to take responsibility for their behavior: we need to face up to what we have and have not done.

I know that such things are difficult. You see, I have unfinished business of my own. And it is not an easy story for me to tell; it's one almost no one knows. But the rabbi's job is not only to teach—it is also to set an example. "One whose learning exceeds his actions," said the great Rabbi Eliezer, "is like a tree whose branches are many but whose roots are few, and the wind comes and plucks it up and throws it upon its face." So I can't just teach others about making things right; I have to try to actually do it myself. Here goes....

Dear Grampa

We like someone because. We love someone although.

HENRI DE MONTHERLANT

Dear Grampa,
    This is not an easy letter for me to write. In a sense, I don't really know you or anything about your life. I'm guessing that you must be about eighty-five years old by now. I know you remarried after Gramma died, and I think you still live in the same house where I last spoke to you almost thirty years ago.
    I want you to know that I remember you. I remember carving pumpkins with you in the basement. You always got the biggest ones for us because you worked in a grocery store. I remember fishing with you in the little creek across the street. I remember watching you eat breakfast—you put ketchup on your scrambled eggs. Yes, I remember pumpkins, fishing, and ketchup on your eggs. I remember you used to call me Stevie—no one else ever did. But that's all I remember.
    We were cut off from each other in some twisted family conflict that I do not understand. Maybe it was about Gramma dying in what I think was a suicide, maybe it was about money, maybe you were wrong, maybe Mom and Dad were wrong, maybe everyone was. It doesn't matter anymore, because I am now a grown man and you are an old man—how much time is left? It doesn't matter anymore because adults have to find the strength to face up to what they have and have not done.
    When people ask me if I have grandparents, I usually say no—preferring that over trying to explain what I do not understand. Sometimes I actually feel as if I have no grandparents; as

if the business between us is finished, all the loose ends neatly knotted. But other times, like when I watch my children play with my parents, I realize I was robbed, and you were too. We never had the chance to grow up together—to fish, roughhouse, and eat ice cream.

Maybe the thing I regret most of all is something you don't even know about. It happened eight years ago when Betsy, our then one-year-old son, Aaron, and I were visiting Mom and Dad in Minneapolis. We were shopping at some discount store when Mom pulled me aside. "Look over there," she whispered, pointing to a small, balding man in bright polyester clothes and a cap. "That's your grandfather." You were there, Grampa, less than twenty feet away from me. You were there, and I—torn between loyalties to my mother and the urge to speak, to call you "Grampa" and let you hold your great-grandson—I did nothing. Twenty feet away from so much unfinished business, I did nothing.

How many times has each of us failed to walk those twenty feet to our unfinished business? Twenty feet away from the stack of unread books. Twenty feet away from the exercise bike. Twenty feet from the telephone, from our brother or sister, our kids, our marriages, and our friendships evaporating from neglect. Twenty feet away from all the unfinished business in our lives, and we do ... nothing. Oh, I know that some unfinished business can never be resolved—there's no sin in that. It's not trying that's the shame.

Grampa, you have no idea how much I regret not walking those twenty feet in that store to say hello to the small, balding man in the bright polyester clothes and a cap. To call you "Grampa" and let you hold your great-grandson. So I'm sending you this letter and a promise to visit when I reach Minneapolis in April. And I'm making myself a promise that this year's Yom Kippur prayers will be more than prayers, that this year will be different. For you, for me, for all of us.

See you in April,
Stevie

Dear Grampa,

Just a note to thank you for the photos. You cannot imagine how much it meant to me to visit, to see pictures of cousins and family I have never really known—most of all the pictures of your brother Sollie, after whom I was named, and of your grandfather Shulem Zelig, after whom Sollie was named—you have solved a five-generation puzzle that I have wondered about for most of my life.

Seeing you again was both more and less than I expected. What I mean by less than I expected is that it was so much less frightening to pick up the phone, to drive to your home and walk in the front door than I ever imagined it would be—it was natural and right. What was more than I expected was the degree to which seeing you has lifted this nagging, unspoken burden I have carried for most of my life. I have a bridge to my childhood, I have a history, I have a grandfather—connections that everyone deserves and that I suspect almost everyone can have if they just pick up the phone, call, write, visit, ignore the barriers. However much we stay in touch, I want you to know that I think of you often and walk more solidly upon the earth because I feel more whole, more connected, more loved. Thanks again for the pictures. Let's talk soon.

Dear Mom

The Mother's heart is the child's school room.

HENRY WARD BEECHER

Dear Mom,

I write to you again this Mother's Day. But this time, a little wiser and more grateful for you; more grateful because now I have two children of my own. Watching each of our babies emerge, seeing how they burst into the waiting world in a sheer, painful, exquisite act of will—knowing how badly they were wanted, how miraculous their journey, has taught me about you and your love for me.

Some days, I think of Betsy and myself as heroes for trying to raise two kids; then I remember that you and Dad raised five. I took out my calculator and did a little figuring:

At six per day, for two years per child, you changed 27,375 diapers.

You made over one hundred fifty trips to the pediatrician, not to mention the dermatologists, allergists, and orthodontists.

At three per year per child for eighteen years, you bought over three hundred pairs of shoes, not to mention skates, cleats, and flippers.

At even just two meals a day, six days a week per family member for each of the years any of us kids lived at home, you served 183,960 plates of food. Not including all the school lunches you packed or the years that our relatives who were fleeing the Communist takeover in Chile lived with us—making it eleven for dinner every night.

I hear a lot of jokes about Jewish princesses, about how spoiled and selfish Jewish women are. None of them make sense when I think of you. Having my own children, I now look back at your life as a young parent, and I know that the money wasn't always there, that Dad couldn't be home much, that you drank five cups of coffee a day just to keep going. I know that you often suffered blinding headaches, that your parents were of no help to you, and that you put a lot of your own wants aside to keep a husband, five kids, relatives, several dogs, birds, fish, frogs, and salamanders so well fed, so well cared for, so well loved.

By the way, I realize that, tough as it was, the cooking, cleaning, and schlepping was the easy part.... The hard part was trying to raise your children to be—for lack of a better word— mensches. I'm not sure how you did it, Mom, but watching Betsy with our two children has given me a clue—I think it boils down to sheer and constant love.

Do you remember the time I played airplane pilot on your sewing machine and accidentally turned it into a mass of broken parts and tangled thread? Or when, as an awkward sixteen-year-old, I mistook the accelerator for the brake and accidentally drove your car through the garage and into the kitchen?

"He thought it was a drive-in restaurant," you joked with family and friends. You made me feel so much better, so much less foolish. You always forgave my awkwardness, Mom. You were my refuge from the pressures and agonies of a world founded upon performance. Even now, I can come to you with my failures, my bruised ego, my skinned and scraped self-image, and know I'm still your little boy, still worthy, still safe.

You know what else I loved about you when I was growing up, Mom? You always believed me, even when I was lying. Through getting arrested for shoplifting, getting kicked out of camp for smoking, rock and roll bands in the basement, failing algebra, fracturing Tommy Murphy's collarbone, having my heart broken at twenty-two by a woman I loved, three months later dating a poet fifteen years older than I, and then a year later dating a female bodybuilder, followed by my surprise engagement to Betsy on our second date, you believed in my goodness.

You always believed I would somehow turn out right. Your faith in me demanded my own self-respect. Your trust made me want to do the right thing even when I wasn't being my best. How does a son thank his mother for believing in him? The older I become, the more I watch my own children, the more I realize what a difference your faith in me made, what a difference your love has made in my life.

Maybe my letter to you will be my message to the congregation this Mother's Day. A little reminder to thank God for a mother's love, for your love, for mothers everywhere. Because it seems to me that the truly lost and lonely in this nervous, unkind world of ours—the shattered and the hopeless among us—got that way because they never had what you managed to give every one of your children: the certainty, the warmth, the breath of unfailing love.

Happy Mother's Day, Mom. I love you.

Dear Dad

. . . a parent's love isn't to be paid back;
it can only be passed on.

HERBERT TARR

Dear Dad,

Tomorrow is Father's Day, and we are thousands of miles apart; apart as we are too often and for too long. So, it seems a good time to write you and tell you—dear God, what to tell you? How can a son possibly say what a father means to him—how can I say what you mean to me?

From the time I was a little boy, I always knew you were different. You didn't play ball like other dads. You didn't help with homework. You didn't cook burgers on Sunday afternoon. I never really understood why until much later. Later I learned that there had been no time for sports, or even school, when you were growing up. You grew up poor; burning-wax-paper-to-stay-warm-in-the-Minnesota-winter poor, picking-tin-cans-out-of-the-garbage-dump poor. I learned that when you were young and would come home from school with a book, the laughter and ridicule was too much for a little boy to take. "Look at the professor," they would say.

So you could never be the Little-League-coaching, algebra-tutoring kind of dad. But we had other things:

Fishing. God, how I loved to fish with you. Watching you row the boat across the lake, shirt off, tan, strong, eyes sparkling like the water. You were a giant; you were my dad. We had long walks in the woods. Smelling, tasting, feeling the wonder of God's great, green earth. We had work. If there was one thing you were going to teach your children, it was work.

When I was young, I never really noticed that you came home with bloody hands and frost-bitten toes, wounds from the war you waged for forty years at Leder Brothers' Scrap Iron and Metal. I never considered the fear and responsibility you must have shouldered. Married at eighteen, with five children to feed by the time you were thirty—yes, work, work was your salvation. Or so I thought. Now I know better. Now I know you were never working for yourself. To this day, in spite of your success, you have a hard time spending money. You were working for me, for Mom, Marilyn, Sherry, Joanne, and Greg too.

I started cleaning toilets and mopping floors at the scrap yard when I was still a little boy. "You have to start at the bottom," you told me. When I got caught shoplifting, you had three truckloads of dirt dumped on our driveway, handed me a wheelbarrow and shovel, and ordered, "Spread it over the yard, front and back." It took an entire summer. It was punishment, a humbling reminder, and it worked. I turned around that summer. Hard work was your salvation, and somehow, it had become mine. It still is and will always be. Can I ever thank you enough for teaching me about the salvation of a job well done?

We never talked much about women, but somehow I grew up respecting women because you always demanded I respect my sisters and my mother. We never talked much about Judaism, but you brought me to shul with you to say Kaddish for your father. You sent me to Israel when I was sixteen, and when we said good-bye at the airport, it was only the second time I ever saw you cry.

We never talked much about education, ideas, or the world, but from the time I was a little boy, you said, "There's always money for books." Later, you sent me off to Oxford to study Shakespeare, to tour Europe and Russia. You supported me through college and five years of graduate school. The boy who was teased by his immigrant parents for wanting to read became the father whose mantra was "There's always money for books."

We never talked much about tzedakah, but somehow you were always helping someone who had much less. We never talked much about family, but you raised five children who live today without sibling rivalry because we had a father who knew how to forgive. *Somehow you managed to rework your worldview to embrace a son, my brother, who is gay. Somehow, even now, you manage to guide your children without ever telling them what to do.*

We never talked much about marriage, but at our wedding toast, you looked at Betsy and me, raised your glass with a wide smile, and simply said, "May you always be each other's best friend." After all these years of performing weddings myself, of premarital counseling with hundreds of couples, of volumes read on love and marriage, leave it to you to have said exactly the right thing. Leave it to you to get to the heart of it all in one sentence.

We never talked much about being a mensch, but never once did I see you favor rich over poor, beautiful over ordinary, Jew over non-Jew, man over woman, white over black. We never talked much about being a father, but somehow, thanks to your example, I feel like I'm getting it right with my own children.

You know, Dad, there's a story in the Torah about when Aaron, the High Priest, is about to die. He takes off his priestly vestments and puts them on his son El'azar. It's our tradition's way of saying we must carry on the work of our fathers, that eventually they live through us. Lately I've noticed something about us, Dad. We never used to, but now we end every phone call by saying "I love you." I think it's because somehow we sense that ever so slowly, we're getting closer to Aaron and El'azar; closer to the end than we are to the beginning.

So I'm writing to say thank you, Dad. Thank you for teaching me about God's green earth, hard work, women and friendship, money for books, and being a mensch. Thank you for being the man I will forever strive to become, for getting me ready to carry on your work. Happy Father's Day.

Love, Steve.

Dear Greg

*In my view, the Jewish condemnation of
homosexuality is the work of human beings—
limited, imperfect, fearful of what is different
and, above all, concerned with ensuring tribal
survival. In short, I think our ancestors were
wrong about a number of things, and
homosexuality is one of them.*

RABBI JANET MARDER

Dear Greg,

*I want you to know that even if you were not my brother, I
would still love you like a brother. I love your heart, your wisdom,
your laughter, the sparkle in your beautiful blue eyes, and your
courage in the face of a world, a people, and yes, sometimes a
family—our family—that stands against you.*

*It has been more than ten years since Mom cornered me in
the small kitchen of our suburban Minnesota home and asked
me in fear and anger, "Is your brother gay?"*

"Why don't you ask him?" I answered.

*But bearing down on me with every bit of muscle and
intimidation her four-foot-eleven-inch body could muster, she
said with restrained rage, "I am asking you!"*

*You and I had prepared for this day. Years before, you had
shared your secret with me, and I had protected it and you from
our family with all my might. But we knew this day would come.*

*For our sisters, it was a suspicion confirmed and little more.
But for our mother—fragile and sometimes worn out by life—it
meant vomiting and migraines. For our father, who lived in a*

blue-collar world of diesel trucks and fag jokes, it meant months, even years, of silent sorrow behind a mask of acceptance.

And for you, my dear brother, it meant allowing your family into what had already been a decade of courageous war. The depression, the anxiety attacks, the abuse, the loneliness, the cemeteries—mourning young men lost too soon to a virus too cruel for words—the lost jobs, the awkward family pictures, all of it would have destroyed a weaker soul. But not you. Instead, you became our family's teacher...my teacher.

From you, I have learned that coming out leads at first to shattering disappointment to and from your loved ones. But that disappointment is nothing like the torture of living a lie. You have taught me about a community of men and women who love and celebrate one another like none I have ever witnessed. From you, I have learned to laugh at straight people, including myself. We are too straight—prisoners of our own narrow vision.

I know what the Torah says about homosexuality: it's called an "abomination punishable by death." But I don't believe it; I believe this must have been written by well-meaning yet ignorant human beings who could not see that a loving God would never have desired such a thing. It could only have come from people who knew almost nothing of what we know today; people who did not know the goodness and deep Jewish soul of my brother Greg.

It's a serious thing for a rabbi to say that the Torah is wrong. But we say it about slavery, which the Torah allows. We say it about concubinage and polygamy, which the Torah allows. And so I say it, too, about being gay.

I know that because our tradition and others call homosexuality an abomination, some people never come out. I know that teenage boys and girls slash their own wrists because they are afraid. I know that fag-bashing is sport in some American towns. These are the real abominations.

I know that some people believe their family will never be up to the challenge of accepting and then loving a gay child, brother, *or sister. But I also know that because of you, our family has learned slowly, over the years, how to be a family—a real family that loves from a place so much deeper and more honest than before.*

So, thank you for trusting me enough to know that I would love you always, for believing that Mom and Dad would also find their way to a place of love. Thank you, my brother, my teacher, for your heart, your wisdom, your laughter, your deep Jewish soul, for the sparkle in your beautiful blue eyes. . .for your courage.

I love you.

Steve.

CHAPTER 8

Death

A bereaved woman came to the rabbi and told him that her bereavement had robbed her of all peace of mind, while her friends' efforts at consolation merely increased her sorrow.

The rabbi advised her to bake a cake, using ingredients gathered only from inhabitants of the town who had never experienced sorrow or grief.

The anguished woman went from house to house, but in each case, she was unable to accept even a single grain of wheat. That night, weary with disappointment, she returned to the rabbi to report her failure.

Suddenly it dawned on her that the failure was the remedy. She realized that she had not been singled out but rather that sorrow is the fate of all mortals.

TRADITIONAL STORY

MY FIRST DATE WITH the woman who is now my wife lasted twelve hours. We started with dinner and ended up talking until the sun rose over the Ohio River the next morning. What made Betsy so interesting to me and made me fall in love with her almost immediately was more than her perfect azure eyes and her shy smile. It was her suffering.

At the time, my heart was broken from a long, difficult relationship with another woman. Somehow Betsy seemed to understand pain and heartache; she seemed wise beyond her years. When the wind blew, I discovered why. The breeze moved Betsy's hair enough for me to realize that the back of her head was basically bald.

"I lost it from radiation," she told me. Betsy went on to explain that she had just recently finished treatment for Hodgkin's disease, a dangerous but curable cancer. So that was it; that was where her honest, wise approach to life was rooted—in her cancer. People who have struggled are more interesting, more grown-up, and have more to say than people who walk through life unwounded. They are less wasteful of time and love, less foolish and confused. Sure, it would be nice to have wisdom with ease, but I haven't yet met the person who does. Insight is wrestled from adversity.

Think back to the most famous wrestling match in the Torah. Jacob is asleep in the desert, waiting to meet his brother, Esau, after twenty years. He dreams about a man/angel who wrestles with him throughout the night. Jacob has struggled with many things in his life since deceiving his father and his brother some twenty years earlier, but he has never encountered anything like this.

According to the Torah, since the all-night bout seems to be a draw, the man/angel tries one final tactic, wrenching

The Extraordinary Nature of Ordinary Things

Jacob's hip socket to cause a permanent limp. Don't get the wrong idea, though; Jacob is no pushover. As dawn finally approaches, Jacob is in the power position, and the man/angel begs to be set free. "I will not let you go unless you bless me," Jacob demands.

The man/angel agrees and blesses Jacob by telling him, "Your name shall no longer be Jacob but Israel, for you have striven with beings divine and human, and have prevailed." With that, Jacob awakes, alive but wounded, both defeated and victorious, transformed from a mere man into the father of our people and nation. After a life of disappointment and sorrow, Jacob, now Israel, is finally blessed.

Interpreting dreams is always risky. Most rabbis play it fairly safe by turning Jacob's subconscious wrestling match with the man/angel into an allegory about Jews ultimately triumphing over their oppressors. But I think Jacob's dream three thousand years ago points to a deeper truth—the same truth Betsy possessed and the same truth revealed in this article by Helen Ravenhill. Actually, it's more a list than an article, and it's called:

Things I Never Thought I'd Know before October 7, 1995

1. The best wig shop.
2. The most appealing way to tie a turban.
3. That a double mastectomy just plain hurts.
4. That my husband wouldn't mind emptying my drains.
5. What I look like with short hair.
6. What I look like with no hair.
7. That I can lift weights and not just the remote.
8. Postcancer immodesty—I've lifted my shirt to many women in the same game.
9. Who invented Compazine and how much I want to kiss them.

10. Too much chicken soup is too much chicken soup.
11. I do great laundry, but most of my friends can do my laundry great too, once I let them.
12. There is no finer man in America than my husband.
13. That I can't exist without my family and my friends.
14. Speaking out about how I feel, have felt, or will feel is the way to go.
15. Breast cancer is the best thing that ever happened to me.

Helen's list is about what adversity teaches. A lot of people could make their own list—the alcoholic who gave up drinking, the man sexually abused as a child or a woman who's been raped, those who've lost their home, their money, their reputation, or their child, anyone who has gone on after gently lowering a loved one's body into the silent ground—they know what trouble and mourning bring if you hold on long and hard enough.

The most important lessons can only be learned through struggle: until you have been disappointed by life, you will never know humility or fearlessness. To really understand that—as one young heart patient with three small children put it to me, "Even a bad day is a gift"—you have to have faced the possibility of running out of days.

In the Torah, Jacob became Israel only after being wounded; he had to fight for his blessing. Helen had to lose her breasts to find herself; Betsy her hair; all of us, sooner or later, the people we love. Everyone gets wounded. We all walk through life with some kind of limp. The Torah's challenge is for us to be like Jacob, wrestling meaning and purpose from our sorrow; recognizing that within our wounds is pain but so, too, the secret to becoming truly blessed.

Room 4913

There is an ever-rotating wheel in this world.

MIDRASH RABBAH

It was the kind of call a rabbi, especially a young rabbi, fears. "Rabbi, my mother is dying," Paulette sobbed. "It could be any minute now. Please come. Cedars Sinai, room 4913. Cancer. Breast, colon, now liver and lung. Soon, Rabbi, soon."

As I drove to the hospital, I reviewed the proper prayers to be said in the presence of the dying. That much rabbinical school had prepared me for. But what about the rest? What else to say? What meaning and purpose could be found? What comfort? What sense?

I entered the room expecting the worst and found it. Vivian, a once beautiful and vibrant woman with sparkling eyes and thick, brown hair, was now little more than a skeleton; her body, awkward and frail. Her head was bald and spotted from brutal chemotherapy; her skin, brittle and transparent; her eyes, dull and milky white. Worst of all, her mouth was twisted, forced upward in a horrible gape. An empty rattle came from deep in her failing lungs. A gasp. A shudder.

Vivian's daughter and I stayed with her for two-and-a-half hours in that cheerless hospital room. The unsteady, raspy breathing served as a constant background to our whispered conversation. We talked a lot about Vivian. Her life. Its tragedies and victories. About how much she would be missed, how unfair and cruel this cancer had been. Most of all, we talked about how lonely Paulette would be when her mother was finally gone.

We also talked about the future. About how death can come as a friend and leave behind more than mere sadness.

About the challenge, the ideals, the aspirations that Vivian was leaving behind for her only daughter to fulfill.

Finally, when I could stay no longer, with one arm around the trembling young woman's shoulder, and the other grasping ever so gently the thin, bony fingers of the old woman, now more creaturelike than human, robbed of her dignity, clinging to life in the most weak and terrible way, I asked, "Do you know the Sh'ma?" Paulette nodded, and together, amid the tortured breathing, we said, *"Sh'ma Yisrael Adonai Eloheinu Adonai Echad.* Hear, O Israel. Adonai is our God. Adonai is One."

A strange and mystical power filled the tiny room. For one brief second, we each understood our place in this vast universe. Vivian was to die. I was to give that death a Jewish voice that connected it to generations long past and yet to come. Paulette was to live on, to transcend the pain of the moment with the profound knowledge that she was the only person in the world who could keep alive what was in her mother's soul.

Such an afternoon weighs heavily upon any rabbi. But perhaps more so upon me at the time. My wife was pregnant with our first child, and I had been thinking a lot about parents and children, about life and death, about what we really leave behind when we die. Somehow that hospital visit brought it all together.

When I arrived home, I hugged Betsy tighter and longer than usual. Then I put my head on her stomach to feel the life within. I studied a lot of theology and philosophy in rabbinical school. But until that hospital visit, I never really understood love or life. Now I know that love creates life...that our lives, and perhaps our deaths, have meaning mostly because of our children.

For whatever hopes and dreams we cherish, whatever light and vision we may bring to this world, they are only impermanent dreams, distant lights, and incomplete visions. We will all die too soon. Before the Messiah comes. Before all the hungry are fed and the homeless sheltered. Before every poem is written and every prayer uttered in piety. Before the world is a gentle place where people speak with wisdom on their lips.

That is the challenge left to our children: to an only daughter trembling in her dying mother's room or an unborn baby waiting to take its place among our people. It's the challenge left to every Jew, because eventually each of us stands to say Kaddish for parents whose ideals become our inheritance. We stand for God's plan and vision, hints of the truth we glimpse in rooms like 4913.

All Life Is Separation

I am exiting through one door, and I am
entering through another.

BA'AL SHEM TOV

"All life is separation," says my friend whose father died last year just as she was sending her eighteen-year-old triplets off to different colleges and directing a new nursery school full of anxious parents with three-year-olds wrapped around their legs, begging them not to go. Just the other day, my own daughter pleaded with me—teary eyes, drippy nose, and outstretched arms—not to leave her on the playground at school. After forty-five minutes of reasoning, I finally said, "Hannah, I know it's sad when Daddy leaves. It's okay to be sad. Goodbye."

Afterward, I came home to write about the Torah portion in which God commands Abram, the first Jew, to leave his country, his relatives, and his home in pursuit of an unknown land and an unknown religion. He arrives in Canaan only to be forced out by famine. Next, Abram flees to Egypt to escape the famine and later returns to Canaan. Once there, he says goodbye to his nephew, Lot, and sends him on his own way.

Then, God appears in a vision, telling Abram his descendants will become strangers in a "land not their own" for four hundred years. Finally, Abram undergoes circumcision and learns that every eight-day-old Jewish boy will be handed over by his parents to a mohel and circumcised—acknowledging that the baby belongs not only to his parents but also to a people and to God. In the next Torah portion, Abraham is commanded to sacrifice his own son.

Sitting at my desk, thinking back on my crying daughter at the playground and Abram's life some three thousand years ago, my friend's words returned to me—"all life is separation."

I'm not one to idealize separation—it hurts. Anyone who's had a pet put to sleep or just handed a set of car keys to their sixteen-year-old knows that even ordinary goodbyes can be painful. The tears in parents' eyes are always bittersweet at a bris, bar or bat mitzvah, graduation, or wedding. Playgrounds, airports, dorms, hospitals, front door steps, cemeteries —all are full of painful goodbyes.

It's always impressed me that Judaism mandates that goodbyes be said with a certain amount of hope. We end Shabbat with *havdalah*, a beautiful ceremony concluded by extinguishing a twisted candle in sweet wine and singing a song asking for a week of peace and a time of redemption for humankind. Seders end with the promise, "Next year in Jerusalem." On Simchat Torah, we conclude the reading of the Torah by rolling back to its beginning. Funerals end with Kaddish, a prayer not about death but about the generous gift of life and God's goodness. At the completion of shiva, the rabbi often takes the mourners out of their home for a brief stroll that enacts literally what is meant symbolically— walking them back into life. Somehow Jews trust that every ending is also a beginning, that the brokenhearted will again feel loved, and the sun will rise no matter how long or dark the night.

Abraham says many painful goodbyes in the Torah. But in return for his losses and his faith, God makes him a promise: "I will make of you a great nation...and you shall be a blessing." With the first Jew on his first journey, the Torah makes it clear that painful endings are important beginnings.

When I picked Hannah up at school that afternoon, she ran to me full of fingerpaint and laughter. The morning's fear and anxiety were long gone, and as she wrapped her little arms around me with all her might, I held her close. She was happy; I was proud. It was a simple, ordinary moment. But in it, we both rediscovered the exquisite truth of Abram and of my friend—all life is separation. Without departure, there can be no arrival; blessings do not come any other way.

A Little Reminder

Not to have had pain is not to have been human.

YIDDISH PROVERB

W hen he was five, I explained the basics of Sukkot to my son, Aaron, for weeks. I told him it was a sort of Jewish Thanksgiving, a weeklong harvest festival. During Sukkot, Jews construct small booths reminiscent of the ones the ancient Israelites dwelled in during their pilgrimages to the Temple in Jerusalem. I told him that we were going to build our own sukkah, just like the ones our ancestors built, and that we were going to eat and sleep in it as the Bible and Talmud command. How much of this Aaron actually understood, I don't know. But the part about sleeping out in the backyard definitely sunk in.

A few days before that Sukkot, we put down the back seats in my wife's van and drove off to a unique L.A. establishment called Feldman's Sukkah Kits. They've been around, as their letterhead proclaims reckoning time according to the Jewish calendar, "since 5739," which is 1979 to most people.

Somehow we maneuvered the long, clumsy box of poles, hardware, fabric, and slats into the car. It hung out the back a little, so we strapped the whole thing down, tied a red flag on the end, buckled ourselves in, and headed for home. Aaron rode shotgun in his safety seat, sunglasses and juice box at the ready. We felt a certain pride in hauling our cargo. It was, I suppose, the modern Jewish equivalent of strapping a freshly killed deer to the bumper. A five-year-old and his dad; two mighty Jewish hunters returning home with their prey.

We had big plans for our sukkah. First, we put it together; my tools were Black and Decker, Aaron's, Fisher-Price. It looked a little rickety when we finished, but that's how everything that I assemble at home looks. Next, it was off to Toys 'R Us to buy a couple of Power Ranger sleeping bags. Then we packed some snacks, popped some corn, mixed up the hot chocolate and poured it in the Thermos, put on our sweats, unrolled the sleeping bags, fired up the flashlights, and hiked right out there in the backyard. The rabbi and his son, urban adventurers.

I had it all planned: We'd have ghost stories and songs, jokes and deep talk about the distant stars and whether or not God put them there, and discussion about why goldfish and grandparents die and where they go when they do. Then we'd sip some hot chocolate and drift off into a peaceful sleep.

Actually, most of the hot chocolate got spilled inside, outside, and underneath the sleeping bags. There were plenty of bathroom breaks and lots of rocks underneath the floor of the sukkah. Cats came around and made scary noises. Birds sang but not so sweetly. The automatic sprinklers went off in the middle of the night; we both got soaked; my feet were cold; and there wasn't much talk of goldfish, God, or anything else. Just a couple of guys who'd have been better off in their own beds.

Looking back at it, though, Aaron and I learned a lot from the expedition. It was a little reminder of the cold so we might appreciate warmth. A little fragility so we might appreciate people who give us strength. Some humility and homelessness so we might appreciate the material richness of our lives. A little reminder that even the best sukkah, and even the best life, is fragile and temporary, exposing us sometimes to the cold.

Randy and Sarah

If you would prevail in life, be prepared for death.

SIGMUND FREUD

At the age of twenty-five, Randy crawled up onto her mother Sarah's bed and curled into a fetus-like shape as if back in the womb. Sarah reached out a fragile, bony arm bruised from needles and tubes and stroked her daughter's hair with the last drops of her draining strength. The monitor showed Sarah's breathing was slowing. Each hour, fewer breaths would be hers until there was breath no more. I watched from a corner of the hospital room, a rabbinic partner in this family's death vigil over a woman with only hours left.

Randy and Sarah whispered to each other for most of those last few hours; there were soft tears, a little laughter, and quiet sorrow. I didn't hear much, but what I did hear was mostly about life and love. Sarah talked about her hopes for her daughter and the grandchildren she would never know. Randy just stayed curled on the bed, snuggled up as close as could be, telling her mother over and over again how much she loved her. Then, like a breeze, a shadow, Sarah was gone.

These deathbed goodbyes are something rabbis see a lot of but most families experience only once or twice if they're lucky. I say if they're lucky because, more often than not, our loved ones die without a chance for us to snuggle up and hold on. As surreal and sad as it is, there's something precious about a last kiss on the forehead of the ones who brought us into life; something about those final, whispered words that touches eternity. It may sound strange to the uninitiated, but for others—doctors, hospice nurses, rabbis—seeing people die well is a privilege.

Helping someone you love die well means being with them as much as possible. Even if they tell you to go home, to be with your own children, to "get the hell out," stay anyway. Sit in the corner and read, watch TV, sleep; just be around them a lot. Being there helps them when they are dying and helps you after they're gone. You'll know that you were with them as much as possible and didn't waste any time. Many years later, this will stave off regret and bring you peace.

As hard as it is, when someone you love is dying, they need your help to talk about it. I usually begin the conversation by asking, "Are you scared?" The dying person knows exactly what I am really asking, which is, "Are you afraid of dying?" Usually, the answer is "no." But asking the question opens the door for them to talk. Often people don't want to burden or frighten their family, but they need and want to talk; providing them the opportunity requires courage and love. These can be the most important and beautiful conversations many families ever have.

The most meaningful part of that conversation arrives at the end when you must tell them you'll be okay, that you love them, and, finally, that it's okay to rest, to let go, to die. This is never easy, but it is the final and best gift you can bestow upon them—the gift of peace.

Of course, all of this is possible only if people know roughly when they will die and are aware enough to carry on a conversation—not the kind of information any of us can have in advance. So, best for each of us to choose our last words to our loved ones before the last minute arrives. I know most Jews have material wills. But at death's door, Jews are taught to leave more than a material legacy to our children: we are taught to leave them words…hopes. In fact, the Hebrew for *words* and *things* is the same—*devarim*. For Jews, words are real, tangible, and valuable.

The nonmaterial inheritance of the words we leave our children is called an ethical will. Ethical wills began informally almost four thousand years ago with Jacob, when he gathered his sons around him to bless them with his dying words. Written ethical wills date back to eleventh century Germany, France, and Spain. There are volumes of them.

We spend so much of our time accumulating wealth and possessions to leave behind for our children, as if the material will somehow express to them the emotional. Why not also follow Jacob's example and that of other Jews for almost a millennium and leave our children a written account of our hopes and love for them? I started my ethical will a few months ago. It's a work in progress, but I offer it as a humble example:

Dear Aaron and Hannah,

Most of all, I want you to know that you and your mother are the joy of my life; all other accomplishments pale in comparison. I want you always to be good Jews, because then I know you will be good, charitable, loving, disciplined, decent people.

Live more for today than for tomorrow. Be forgiving to a fault. When you do something, do your very best. Tell many jokes, both dirty and clean. Always try to have enough money so that you are never afraid of someone else's power over you. But use your money to help the needy.

Never pick a fight. But if someone picks one with you, don't back down. If you have done someone good...see it as a small thing. If someone has done you wrong...see that as a small thing too. See the world, dance, and give. Let good food, warm bread, and wine grace your table. Study Torah diligently. Be welcome in each other's homes. Light a yahrtzeit candle for your mother and me when we are gone.

Most of all, remember that I love you deeply and forever.

Dad

You can use this ethical will as a starting place, or use someone else's, or start completely on your own with a pencil and a sheet of paper—but write one. Your children will need your wisdom and your words more than any possession you can leave them...especially if you and they never get the chance Randy and Sarah had to snuggle up and say goodbye.

The Pen of Our Lives

Some who live are dead, and some who are dead
still live.

PHILO

I n rabbinical school, we had a class on how to write
sermons, wedding addresses, and eulogies. One day, the
professor took out the obituary section of the newspaper, cut
it into pieces, and put the pieces in a hat. Our assignment was
to write a eulogy for the person whose obituary we pulled out
of the hat. Obituaries don't usually tell you very much. Just
the name, age, surviving family, if any, maybe an occupation.
That meant we had to imagine what the person's life might
have been like. We had to create the details, stories, dreams,
and accomplishments in order to imbue their death with
meaning.

Since then, I've given hundreds of real eulogies. I try hard
every time to say something significant. But any rabbi who's
honest will tell you that not all eulogies are the same. Some
eulogies are a little thin, a bit empty, because some people's
lives are empty. There are, of course, so many eulogies I will
never forget, so many people I will never forget:

There was Gert, who entered USC at sixteen, received an
advanced degree in chemistry, and helped invent the process
for canning fresh fruit. No Gert—no cling peaches.

When it came to golf, Jean simply remarked: "If you can't
be good, be sure you have the right outfit on!" Will her grandchildren ever forget those weekly trips in her big Lincoln to
Delores's for Jumbo Jims?

There was Bob—Harvard Business School, swimming
medals, unimaginable wealth and success, but whose son

remembers him best as the dad who built a cage for his pet "Sally" the salamander.

Ida worked at a bakery. Whenever her grandchildren came in, she took them behind the counter so the bakers could make frosting flowers in the palms of their little hands. Ida smiled as they licked them up with glee.

Harry lost two wives to cancer and never grew bitter.

Pru painted landscapes with so much passion, you could feel the sky.

Lolly kept this poem in her purse:

What counts the most in this old world?

What makes life bright and gay?

What are the most important things that drive our cares away?

They are not wealth or power or the things that gold can buy.

They are the little common things that keep our spirits high.

Like moonbeams dancing through the trees and stars shining above.

The peace and real tranquility we gain from sincere love.

Lolly was 96 when she died.

Although I didn't realize it at the time, that assignment in rabbinical school was a graphic example of an important truth—that each of us holds our own obituary in our hands. Every day we are creating the details, acts of love, stories, visions, and legacy of our lives. The rabbi merely records our eulogy on paper: we write it with the pen of our lives. After you've buried enough people, some more memorable than others, you begin to understand that. You confront the fact that our deaths are really going to be about our lives.

The Wild Thing

People ride, but God holds the reins.

YIDDISH PROVERB

S ooner or later, most of us are willing to make a deal with God; it may be when we discover the lump in our breast or the pain in our chest, when the earth begins to shake, or our marriage starts to crumble. The deal goes something like this: "We'll do better, God. Please...save us. Save the people we love." Consider my friend Gail—a writer and mother—who described her most recent deal with God this way:

At thirty-seven, I, the responsible one, the un-party girl, have broken free—for three minutes anyway. I have ridden the Wild Thing—one of the world's fastest roller coasters. There's no shortage of speculation about my roller-coaster adventure. An early midlife crisis and temporary insanity are the most popular theories among close friends.

How can I tell them the truth? How can I admit that their no-nonsense companion has deliberately, consciously proposed a bargain to some unseen, unknown power? "I'll ride this damn thing. You keep my mother alive," I offer secretly to my private God.

"She can't die," my seven-year-old daughter tells me as I hand her a Popsicle in the kitchen. "Then you wouldn't have any parents."

So what do I tell this precious, inquisitive child named for my father, who died of cancer eight years ago, ten months before her birth? That just because one person you love dies from cells gone mad doesn't protect you from having to face the possibility again? Is it time to pull out the terribly inadequate parenting speech called "life's not fair"?

What does Judaism say to this little girl about her grandmother? Can we ride the roller coaster and change God's
mind? Can we escape the ache of being human by being better
human beings? Those of us longing for the touch of a parent,
a husband, a wife, or a dear, sweet child now gone, who feel
broken and empty, we know that all the righteous living in
the world couldn't have kept our loved ones alive. We know a
deeper, tougher truth.

Our congregation lost a ten-year-old child this year.
Another local congregation lost two kids. Is anyone prepared
to say they died because the quality of their character wasn't
up to God's standards or that their parents somehow deserved
this suffering? Can any one child really be less deserving than
another? Do any of us who mourn deserve the pain? It cannot be.

A spiritual life isn't about avoiding suffering. The ancient
rabbis had to know, because we know, that righteous people
suffer all the time. Life offers no guarantees; there is no deal to
be made with God. If there is any kind of certainty, it's simply
to live a life filled with love so that when sorrow comes, we
are not alone. If you lead a life of reaching out to others, of
forgiveness, prayer, and righteousness, and you lose a loved
one, you will feel the embrace of a comforting community.
"That embrace," as a man who lost his thirty-year-old daughter
put it, "changes nothing but means everything."

My friend Gail, who bargained with God for her mother's
life by riding the Wild Thing, wrote that her mother phoned.
"She's chucking the chemotherapy," Gail says:

> *It makes her too sick, and, besides, who really knows how*
> *much good it'll do anyway? My mom prefers to believe that the*
> *surgery got it all. She wants to live in the present, heal herself*
> *with healthy food, long walks, and the love of her new husband.*
>
> *I am furious at her cowardice, until I realize just how brave*
> *she is. Unlike me, she doesn't need to bargain with some higher*
> *power, doesn't have to stuff herself into a little car for a three-*
> *minute-almost-kill-me ride at the amusement park. She knows*

instinctively, through years of loss and holding on, that we can only do so much. Then we simply have to let go, trust, live.

We're each given a day at a time. It's impossible to know anything more than that for certain. So, as Gail puts it, "We'll hold on white-knuckled to the people we love most...because when it comes to the wild thing called life, that's the most important thing we can do."

Room for the Rest of Us

*The difference between the skeptic and the
believer is frequency of faith and not certitude
of position.*

RABBI IRVING GREENBERG

It was my third funeral of the week, and I was tired of death. I thought this one would be easier than the others, since it was an elderly woman who suffered terribly and truly wanted to die. Her name was Ruth, and her only surviving relatives were her nephew, Harry, and his son, Joel.

So I gathered with Harry, Joel, and a few others at Ruth's grave to talk about her life, to pray, and then lower her body into the silent earth. Joel showed up with an armful of books. Recognizing just what books they were, I was betting on trouble. I could tell that Joel was a recent devotee of the Ba'al Teshuvah movement—a group of formerly nonobservant Jews suddenly or slowly adopting Orthodox-like views and behaviors. It's not that I have anything against people taking their Judaism seriously; it's just that, in the past, I've had a few people carrying books like that challenge me in the middle of a funeral in the most inappropriate way, substituting zeal for knowledge and respect. But Joel was cool—he liked the way the ceremony was handled.

After the funeral, still standing near Ruth's grave, Joel asked if he could read something from one of his books. I nodded. Joel had brought a friend of his along, a young woman whose husband had died just a month ago. Although all of us listened, it was pretty clear that Joel was reading to her. His text? Ezekiel's vision in the Valley of Dry Bones, a miraculous passage in the Bible demonstrating God's ability to resurrect the dead. After he finished, Joel turned to me and said, "This idea of the dead being reborn was the hardest thing for me to accept about Judaism. But then one of the rabbis I study with showed me a lemon seed and said, 'If God can make an orchard grow from this seed, then God can do anything.'"

I was impressed with Joel's fervor but not his logic. "Why," I wanted to ask him, "if God can do anything, didn't God prevent the Holocaust or liver cancer?" But I didn't mess with Joel; it wasn't the time or the place. Besides, his friend was comforted by the thought of seeing her husband again in some messianically resurrected state. I suppose for many, that's enough.

During the car ride back to temple I envied Joel's faith, but I also knew it wasn't in me to ignore all the evil in the world that contradicts it. For most of us, faith comes less easily and surely. We are not all that different from our ancestors in the Torah who, after witnessing God's powerful plagues against the evil Pharaoh, the parted sea, manna from heaven, a cloud to lead them by day and a pillar of fire by night, miracle after miracle, still panic. When Moses is barely half a day late descending from Mount Sinai, after all he and God had done for them, the people build a golden calf and dance around it, claiming, "This is our God."

In one way or another, the theme of the ebb and flow of our ancestors' faith is repeated again and again in the Torah. I think it's the Torah's way of telling us that we don't have to have the unshakable conviction of Joel to be part of the Jewish people. Not that there's anything wrong with that kind of faith—it's just not the only kind of faith. We can all take comfort in knowing that even in the case of the golden calf, God punishes but ultimately forgives and sends Moses back up the mountain to give the people another chance. There is always another chance. Look around. Pay attention. Notice. Life is full of faith and meaning, and countless Sinais to climb. . .not only for those with Joel's faith, but for the rest of us too.

Afterword

A friend recently texted me a picture of myself from when we were in rabbinical school together. He had found it while cleaning out his house before selling that now empty nest and downsizing to a retirement condo. I remember the very moment that picture was taken. Seeing it reminded me of all the raw, unrefined, passionate naivete that defined my youth.

The world has changed a lot since then. Zoom meetings, meals and packages delivered daily to our doorstep, GPS, civilian space travel, and pictures from Mars. Yet, as I reread each essay in this book, I realize the human condition has not changed much, if at all, since it was first published in 1999. Each year when we reread the foundational stories of the Torah, it's pretty clear that people haven't changed much in three thousand years. But new rabbis often see, for the first time, aspects of the world and people's lives that only someone with a front-row seat to life can. I sensed early on from that new perspective that there was no such thing as a small blessing or miracle. All life, even its darkest moments, reveals the sacred. This book was my first attempt to help others see and feel what I saw and felt with my new rabbi eyes: the extraordinary nature of ordinary things.

Back then, I was a very young man, husband, father, writer, and rabbi. My children have since grown into adulthood with their own relationships, passions, and worries. My father is dead after a ten-year journey through Alzheimer's disease. Now, my mother is losing her memory. I have faced the surgeon's scalpel, and Betsy has too. We are living through a pandemic that pierces our societal and personal sense of invulnerability, making us long for and appreciate human touch and freedom like never before. Much like that old photo and the world, things have changed a great deal over time. And much like the human condition, they have changed very little. But as my father would often say in Yiddish, *a bisel iz a plotz*—"a little is a lot." I feel that truth ever more so as I grow older, and time feels more finite than it did for the young man in that picture taken forty years ago.

All these years later, I am still witness to laughter, the glory of nature, steady love, crushing disappointment and pain, loss and wonderment, all of which I tried to capture in this first book and am still trying to capture with every new book I write . . . but with a more seasoned and layered understanding of the view from that front row-seat I still occupy every day. I am not a different person now. I am made of the same material. But that material is weathered and mellowed in hue. It has—I have—a patina that only time and experience can bestow.

Revisiting these essays is a lot like seeing that photograph. A reminder of who I was, still am, and always will be, and also how I have grown. For as long as I remember, I have been interested in the ways the most particular and smallest of experiences reveal the most universal truths. Much like how identifying the tiniest of particles that make up all of matter can paradoxically allow us to see what is most common to all that exists. The daily then and now of our lives are precious gifts, and the future, the most precious of all.

After all these years, Betsy and I still hold hands under the covers each night. I still say, "I love you, Betsy." "I love you too," she still whispers. Then we drift off to sleep with our two snoring dogs between us. We are old and married, but with so much more joy, loss, life, laughter, and love ahead. We have been through so much together. We have learned so much together. So much will change. So little will change. Such is the world. Such is life. And it is all extraordinary. . . .

Steve Leder
Los Angeles, CA
2021